Education in Sub-Saharan Africa

A WORLD BANK STUDY

Education in Sub-Saharan Africa
Comparing Faith-Inspired, Private Secular, and Public Schools

Quentin Wodon

THE WORLD BANK
Washington, D.C.

© 2014 International Bank for Reconstruction and Development / The World Bank
1818 H Street NW, Washington DC 20433
Telephone: 202-473-1000; Internet: www.worldbank.org

Some rights reserved

1 2 3 4   16 15 14 13

This work is a product of the staff of The World Bank with external contributions. Note that The World Bank does not necessarily own each component of the content included in the work. The World Bank therefore does not warrant that the use of the content contained in the work will not infringe on the rights of third parties. The risk of claims resulting from such infringement rests solely with you.

The findings, interpretations, and conclusions expressed in this work do not necessarily reflect the views of The World Bank, its Board of Executive Directors, or the governments they represent. The World Bank does not guarantee the accuracy of the data included in this work. The boundaries, colors, denominations, and other information shown on any map in this work do not imply any judgment on the part of The World Bank concerning the legal status of any territory or the endorsement or acceptance of such boundaries.

Nothing herein shall constitute or be considered to be a limitation upon or waiver of the privileges and immunities of The World Bank, all of which are specifically reserved.

Rights and Permissions

This work is available under the Creative Commons Attribution 3.0 Unported license (CC BY 3.0) http://creativecommons.org/licenses/by/3.0. Under the Creative Commons Attribution license, you are free to copy, distribute, transmit, and adapt this work, including for commercial purposes, under the following conditions:

Attribution—Please cite the work as follows: Wodon, Quentin. 2014. *Education in Sub-Saharan Africa: Comparing Faith-Inspired, Private Secular, and Public Schools.* World Bank Study. Washington, DC: World Bank. doi: 10.1596/978-0-8213-9965-1. License: Creative Commons Attribution CC BY 3.0

Translations—If you create a translation of this work, please add the following disclaimer along with the attribution: *This translation was not created by The World Bank and should not be considered an official World Bank translation. The World Bank shall not be liable for any content or error in this translation.*

All queries on rights and licenses should be addressed to World Bank Publications, The World Bank Group, 1818 H Street NW, Washington, DC 20433, USA; fax: 202-522-2625; e-mail: pubrights@worldbank.org.

ISBN (paper): 978-0-8213-9965-1
ISBN (electronic): 978-0-8213-9966-8
DOI: 10.1596/978-0-8213-9965-1

Cover photo: Community school in Macaci, a suburb of Abidjan, Côte d'Ivoire. © Ami Vitale / The World Bank.

Library of Congress Cataloging-in-Publication Data

Wodon, Quentin.
  Education in Sub-Saharan Africa : comparing faith-inspired, private secular, and public schools / by Quentin Wodon.
      pages cm
  Includes bibliographical references.
  ISBN 978-0-8213-9965-1 (pbk. : alk. paper) — ISBN 978-0-8213-9966-8 (e-book)
  1. Education—Africa, Sub-Saharan. 2. Education and state—Africa, Sub-Saharan. 3. Education—Africa, Sub-Saharan—Statistics. I. Title.
    LA1501.W64 2013
    370.96—dc23

2013023212

Contents

Acknowledgments ix
Abbreviations xi

Overview 1
   Market Share of Private Schools 1
   Reach to the Poor 3
   Private Cost of Education 4
   Satisfaction 6
   Reasons for Choosing Specific Schools 8
   Performance 10
   Conclusion 11

Chapter 1   Introduction 13

Chapter 2   Motivation and Background 17
   Introduction 17
   Comparative Advantage of Faith-Inspired Institutions 20
   Combination of Cross-Country and Country-Specific Work 24
   Conclusion 25
   Note 25

Chapter 3   Data and Methodology 27
   Introduction 27
   Household Survey Data 28
   Qualitative and Small Sample Data Collection 31
   Data Validity and Analysis 32
   Limited Scope of the Study 35
   Conclusion 38
   Notes 39

Chapter 4   Market Share 41
   Introduction 41
   Cross-Country Comparisons 42
   Additional Evidence for Ghana and Burkina Faso 47

	Conclusion	49
	Note	49
Chapter 5	**Reach to the Poor and Vulnerable**	**51**
	Introduction	51
	Cross-Country Evidence	53
	Additional Evidence for Ghana and Burkina Faso	59
	Conclusion	63
	Notes	63
Chapter 6	**Private Cost of Education**	**65**
	Introduction	65
	Cross-Country Evidence	66
	Additional Evidence for Ghana and Burkina Faso	70
	Conclusion	77
Chapter 7	**Satisfaction and Preferences**	**79**
	Introduction	79
	Cross-Country Evidence	81
	Additional Evidence for Ghana and Burkina Faso	84
	Conclusion	95
Chapter 8	**Conclusion**	**97**
Appendix A	Faith and Formal Models of School Choice: An Illustration	101
Appendix B	Rationale for Combining Quantitative and Qualitative Data	105
	Note	107
Appendix C	Identification of Faith-Inspired Schools in Multipurpose National Household Surveys	109
Appendix D	Sample Size for the Qualitative Fieldwork	113
Appendix E	Standard Errors for Statistical Tables	115
Appendix F	Role of Faith-Inspired Institutions in Tertiary Education	117
Appendix G	Detailed Regression Estimates	123
Appendix H	Illegitimate Fees in Service Delivery	131
References		135

Boxes

O.1	Data Sources—Household Surveys	2
O.2	Data Sources—Qualitative Work	8
O.3	Example of Testimonies by Parents	10

Figures

O.1	Market Share of Public, Faith-Inspired and Private Secular Schools	2
O.2	Shares of Students in Private Primary School by Welfare Quintile	5
O.3	Average Private Cost of Schooling by Type of Provider	6
O.4	Satisfaction Rates with the Schooling Received	7

Tables

O.1	Shares of Students in Each Type of School by Welfare Quintile	4
O.2	Private Cost of Schooling per Child for Households	5
O.3	Satisfaction Rates with the Various Types of Schools	7
O.4	Main Reasons for Choosing the School, Qualitative Field Work, 2010	9
2.1	Potential Comparative Advantages and Weaknesses of FISs	22
3.1	Identification of FISs in the Education Modules of Selected Household Surveys	29
4.1	Market Share Estimates from UIS Administrative Data, Education	43
4.2	Market Share Estimates from Multipurpose Surveys, Education	45
4.3	Market Share by Type of Primary School, Burkina Faso	48
4.4	Trends in Primary School Enrolment by Type of School, Burkina Faso	48
5.1	Benefit Incidence for Education by Type of Provider	54
5.2	Enrollment Rates by Type of Schools and Disability Status, Ghana 2003	61
5.3	Impact of Disability on School Enrolment by Type of School, Ghana 2003	62
6.1	Cost of School Fees and PTA Dues in Primary Schools	67
6.2	Cost of School Fees and PTA Dues in Secondary Schools	68
6.3	Cost of Primary Education by Type of School, Divided by 10,000, 2005/06 (GHC)	70
6.4	Selected Correlates of the Cost of Education, Ghana, 2005/06	72
6.5	Reason for Not Attending School in Burkina Faso, Children Aged 7–12 (FCFA)	73
6.6	Average Annual School Expenses per Child, Burkina Faso Fieldwork	73

6.7	School Inputs by Type of School, Burkina Faso 2008/09	75
6.8	Passing Rate in Primary Schools by Grade, Burkina Faso 2008/09	77
7.1	Countries in the Sample with Data on Satisfaction in Education Modules	81
7.2	Satisfaction Rates with Primary Education Services	82
7.3	Satisfaction Rates with Secondary Education Services	83
7.4	Main Reasons for Choosing the School, Qualitative Fieldwork, 2010	84
7.5	Advantages of the School You Selected, Qualitative Fieldwork, 2010	85
7.6	What Should Children Learn at School? Qualitative Fieldwork, 2010	86
7.7	Evaluation of Schools by Parents, Qualitative Fieldwork, Ghana 2010	87
7.8	Reasons for Choosing the School over Other Options, Burkina Faso	89
7.9	Comparison of Various Schools in Burkina Faso, Burkina Faso	90
7.10	Literacy and Numeracy in Primary School, Children Aged 10–15, Ghana	92
7.11	Selected Correlates of Subjective Literacy and Numeracy, Ghana	94
C.1	Multipurpose Household Surveys Used for Cross-Country Comparisons	110
C.2	Identification of the Various Types of Education Facilities	111
D.1	Sample Size for Qualitative Data Collection in Ghana and Burkina Faso	114
E.1	Standard Errors for Means of Dichotomized Variables Under Equal Weights and Simple Random Sampling	116
F.1	Market Share of Various Types of Providers, Tertiary Level	118
F.2	Benefit Incidence by Type of Provider, Tertiary Level	119
F.3	Cost of Tertiary Education by Type of Provider, Local Currencies	120
F.4	Satisfaction with Tertiary Education by Type of Provider	122
G.1	Correlates of the Cost of Education for Households, Ghana, 2005/06	123
G.2	Correlates of Perceptions of Literacy and Numeracy, 10–15 Years Old (Primary), Ghana 2005/06	125
G.3	Correlates of School Enrollment and Impact of Disability, Ghana 2003	127
H.1	Gratifications Paid as a Share of Total Income, Sierra Leone 2003	133
H.2	Share of Households Paying Illegitimate School Fees, Cameroon 2001	134

Acknowledgments

This study was written by Quentin Wodon in part on the basis of background papers coauthored with Franck Adoho, Regina Gemignani, Mari Shojo, and Clarence Tsimpo. It is a product of the Human Development Network at the World Bank. Continuous support and advise were provided by Robin Horn, Harry Patrinos, and Elizabeth King. The peer reviewers were Mathieu Brossard and Deon Filmer. Comments from William Barbieri, William Dinges, Charles Jones, Ritva Reinikka, and Ernest Zampelli were very valuable. Any error or omission in the study remains that of the author only and the views expressed in the study are those of the author only and need not represent those of the World Bank, its Executive Directors, or the countries they represent.

Abbreviations

1-2-3	Enquête 123
CAS	Country Assistance Strategy
CBO	Community-based Organization
CCT	Conditional Cash Transfers
CE1/2	Cours Elémentaire 1/2
CEP	Certificat d'Etudes Primaires
CHA	Christian Health Association
CM1/2	Cours Moyen 1/2
CP1/2	Cours Préparatoire 1/2
CSO	Civil Society Organisation
CWIQ	Core Welfare Indicators Questionnaire
dF/dX	Marginal effect in probit regression
DFID	Department for International Development
DHS	Demographic and Health Survey
DRC	Democratic Republic of Congo
EACVM	Enquête Annuelle sur les conditions de vie des ménages
ECAM2	Enquête Camerounaise Auprès des Ménages II
ECOM	Enquête Congolaise auprès des Ménages pour l'évaluation de la pauvreté
ECOSIT2	Enquête sur la Consommation du Secteur Informel au Tchad II
EICV2	Enquête intégrale sur les conditions de vie des ménages II
ELIM	Enquête Légère Intégrée auprès des Ménages
EMIS	Education Management Information System
ENBC	Enquête Nationale sur le Budget et la Consommation des Ménages
ENV	Enquête sur le Niveau de Vie des Ménages de Côte d'Ivoire
ESPS	Enquête de Suivi de la Pauvreté au Sénégal
FBO	Faith-based Organization
FCFA	Franc CFA
FII	Faith-Inspired Institution or Initiative

FIO	Faith-Inspired Organization
FII	Faith-Inspired School
GDP	Gross Domestic Product
GES	Ghana Education Service
GFSP	Ghana School Feeding Program
GHC	Ghana Cedis (before conversion)
GH¢	Ghana cedi (after conversion)
GLSS	Ghana Living Standard Survey
GLSS5	Ghana Living Standard Survey, Fifth Round
IHS	Integrated Household Survey
HDN	Human Development Network (The World Bank)
IA	Instituteur Adjoint
IAC	Instituteur Adjoint Certifié
IC	Instituteur Certifié
ICSED	International Standard Classification of Education
IEU	Islamic Education Unit
ICRO	Islamic Culture and Relations Organisation
INGO	International Nongovernmental Organisation
IRS	Internal Revenue Service
JHS	Junior High School
KIHBS	Kenya Integrated Household Budget Survey
LCMS	Living Conditions Monitoring Survey
LSS	Living Standards Survey
MDG	Millennium Development Goal
MICS	Multiple Indicators Cluster Survey
MoE	Ministry of Education, Science and Sports
MoU	Memorandum of Understanding
NEA	National Eligibility Assessment
NGO	Nongovernmental Organization
ODI	Overseas Development Institute
OECD	Organization for Economic Co-operation and Development
OVC	Orphans and Vulnerable Children
PASEC	Programme on the Analysis of Education Systems
PETS	Public Expenditure Tracking Survey
PPP	Public-Private Partnership
PPP	Purchasing Power Parity
PSU	Primary Sampling Unit
PTA	Parent-Teacher Association
QUIBB	Enquête Questionnaire des Indicateurs de Base du Bien-être

RCT	Rational choice theory
RME	Religious and Moral Education
SHS	Senior High School
SHIES	Swaziland Household Income and Expenditure Survey
SLIHS	Sierra Leone Integrated Household Survey
TVET	Technical and Vocational Education and Training
UIS	UNESCO Institute of Statistics
UNESCO	United Nations Educational, Scientific and Cultural Organization
UNFPA	United Nations Population Fund
UNHS	Uganda National Household Survey
UNICEF	United Nations Children's Fund
UK	United Kingdom
US	United States
USAID	United States Agency for International Development
WFP	World Food Program
WVS	World Values Survey

Overview

Within the context of the Millennium Development Goals (MDGs), donors and governments have made improvements in human development a key priority. Public sector service providers continue to have a leading role in efforts to improve education outcomes, but private providers, including faith-inspired schools (FISs), may also contribute. Given that many developing countries may miss the education targets of the MDGs, it is all the more important for donors as well as national and local governments to recognize the role played by FISs, and where appropriate to support them in their service delivery activities, especially when they reach the poor. Yet in-depth empirical assessments of the role that FISs play in providing education services have not been conducted to-date. The objective of this book is to contribute to an assessment of the role of FISs in education service delivery in Africa. This synthesis of the book briefly discusses the data used for the analysis and presents the main results in terms of the market share of FISs and other private providers, the extent to which they reach to the poor, the private costs for households of their services and the satisfaction with the services provided, and the reasons why some households choose faith-inspired providers.

Market Share of Private Schools

What is the market share of private education service providers in Africa, and within private providers, what is the contribution of faith-inspired and secular providers? In order to answer this question, data from household surveys distinguishing public, faith-inspired and private secular schools from 16 countries were analyzed (see Box O.1 on the data sources). A number of key findings emerge from the analysis:

Finding #1: Faith-inspired schools enroll 14 percent of all primary school students and 11 percent of secondary school students. For secular private secular schools, the shares are 11 percent and 16 percent.

Key results are provided in figure O.1. The average market share for FISs in primary schools in the 16 countries is at 14 percent, versus 12 percent for secular private schools. Public schools account for 74 percent of all schools. The situation is however very different depending of the country. The market shares for FISs

Box O.1 Data Sources—Household Surveys

This study is based on multipurpose and nationally representative household surveys implemented in 16 Sub-Saharan African countries. The choice of countries was based on data availability, using surveys with education modules that identify whether children go to public, faith-inspired, or private secular schools. Information in some of the surveys is also available on the cost of education for households, as well as on the satisfaction of parents with the education received by their children and the reasons for nonsatisfaction.

The 16 countries and corresponding household surveys used for this study are as follows: Burkina Faso (EACVM-QUIBB 2007); Burundi (QUIBB 2006); Cameroon (ECAM 2007); Democratic Republic of Congo (123 survey 2004/05); Ghana (two surveys: CWIQ 2003 and GLSS5 2005/2006); Kenya (KIHBS 2005); Malawi (HIS-2 2004); Mali (ELIM-QUIBB 2006); Niger (ENBC 2007); Nigeria (LMS 2003/2004); ROC (ECOM-QUIBB 2005); Senegal (ESPS 2005); Sierra Leone (SLIHS 2003); Swaziland (SHIES 2009); Uganda (UNHS 2010); and Zambia (LCMS IV 2004).

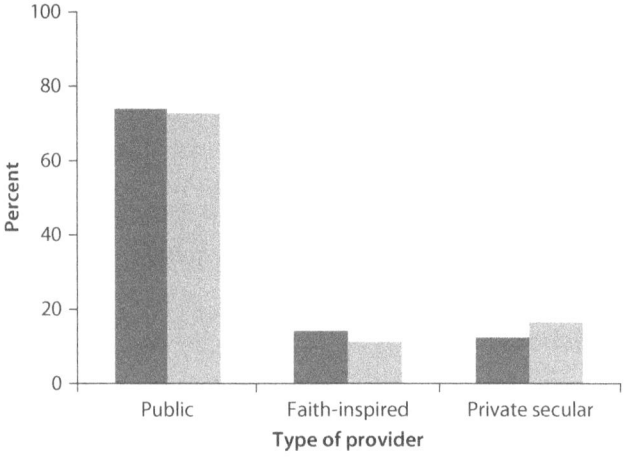

Figure O.1 Market Share of Public, Faith-Inspired and Private Secular Schools
percent (average across the countries)

Source: Tsimpo and Wodon 2013b.

range from 1.2 percent in Mali to 69.8 percent in the Democratic Republic of Congo (DRC). The high market share in the Democratic Republic of Congo (and Sierra Leone) relates in part to conflict that led to state failure and poorly functioning public schools, but also to historical factors. Beyond these two countries, the highest market share for FISs in the 16 countries is at 25.7 percent in Swaziland.

What about secondary education? Mali is again the country with the smallest market share, and the highest market share is obtained for the Democratic

Republic of Congo. The average market share for FISs is at 11.2 percent, versus 16.2 percent for private secular schools and 73 percent for public schools.

How do the market share estimates obtained in this study compare with administrative data? A recent UNESCO Institute of Statistics (UIS) publication provides estimates of the share of enrollment in private schools at both the primary and secondary levels circa 1999 and 2009 (UNESCO 2011). In the UIS report, private schools are defined as those schools that are controlled and managed by a private body such as a nongovernmental organization, a religious body, a special interest group, a foundation, or a business enterprise. Both nonprofit and for-profit schools are considered. Thus, what defines the public/private status of a school is who controls and manages the school, not who funds the school. Privately managed or controlled schools that are funded by the government are considered as private.

For 2009, UIS data are available for 35 countries. The market share of private schools is below five percent in 11 countries, and above 15 percent in nine countries. The average market share for all countries with data in 2009 is 12.8 percent (simple average not weighted by country populations). For the countries with data in 1999, the average private market share is 16.6 percent, but this is driven up by Zimbabwe (without Zimbabwe, the average private market share is 14.3 percent). At the secondary level, the average private market share in 2009 for the countries with data is at 20.0 percent, while it was at 25.0 percent for the year 1999, but this is again due in large part to data available for Zimbabwe in 1999, but not in 2009.

Finding #2: The order of magnitude of the market share of private schools is similar in surveys and administrative data, but it is slightly higher in surveys, possibly in part because some private schools operate without official recognition.

For the countries where estimates are available from both the household surveys used in this study and the UIS data, the average difference in the estimates of private market share is 3.9 percent at the primary level, so that there is a relatively good correspondence in the data. The average private market share observed in the surveys is higher than the average share reported to the UIS by Ministries of Education, and this is what one would expect. Indeed, it is likely that some schools that do provide services to households are not recorded by Ministries of Education, because they operate without any official recognition.

Reach to the Poor

Do faith-inspired schools reach the poor? One way to answer this question is to assess whether in their own clientele, FISs serve the poor—as defined on the basis of their consumption or wealth—more than other groups. Table O.1 shows that 16 percent of students in faith-inspired schools come from households in the bottom quintile of the distribution of welfare, versus 25.3 percent from the top quintile (each quintile accounts for 20 percent of the population). Thus, faith-inspired

Table O.1 Shares of Students in Each Type of School by Welfare Quintile
percent (average across the countries)

	Welfare quintiles				
	Q1	Q2	Q3	Q4	Q5
	Primary schools				
Public	21.7	21.8	21.6	19.9	15.0
Faith-inspired	16.0	17.7	19.5	21.5	25.3
Secular	8.5	11.8	14.2	21.6	43.9
Total	20.0	20.7	20.8	20.3	18.2
	Secondary schools				
Public	12.3	15.7	19.0	23.8	29.2
Faith-inspired	10.4	10.9	20.7	23.1	34.9
Private secular	4.5	8.2	13.2	19.1	54.9
Total	11.2	14.6	18.1	23.3	32.8

Source: Tsimpo and Wodon 2013b.

schools tend to serve the poor slightly less than the better off. This is not surprising because the cost of education is often high for the poor, resulting in lower demand than among the better-off, especially when cost recovery is prevalent as is the case with faith-inspired schools that do not benefit from public funding.

Finding #3: Faith-inspired schools tend to reach the poor slightly less than public schools, but much more than private secular schools.

How do FISs compare to public facilities? The benefit incidence by quintile for FISs is less pro-poor than for public facilities, for both primary and secondary schools. Indeed, for public facilities 21.7 percent of children come from the bottom quintile at the primary level, and the share is 12.3 percent at the secondary level versus 10.4 percent for faith-inspired schools. On the other hand, as expected, the services provided by faith-inspired schools are less tilted towards better-off children than is the case for private secular schools, for which 43.9 percent of the students in primary schools and 54.9 percent of the students in secondary schools come from households belonging to the top quintile. Thus it is clear from table O.1 that faith-inspired schools serve the poor more than private secular schools, as also shown in figure O.2.

Private Cost of Education

The question of the extent to which FISs and private secular schools reach the poor is closely related to the cost for households of the services provided, and the amount of funding available to the schools. In some cases, FISs may benefit from special resources to make services more affordable for the poor, for example when they get support from congregations, whether these are locally based or located in developed countries, or from other organizations including government agencies. In the absence of such support, subsidies granted to the poor may require charging better-off patients more for the

Figure O.2 Shares of Students in Private Primary School by Welfare Quintile

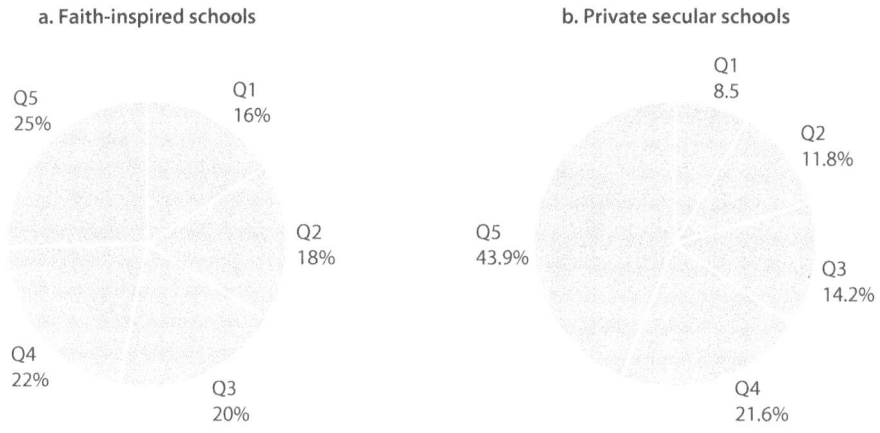

a. Faith-inspired schools
- Q1 16%
- Q2 18%
- Q3 20%
- Q4 22%
- Q5 25%

b. Private secular schools
- Q1 8.5
- Q2 11.8%
- Q3 14.2%
- Q4 21.6%
- Q5 43.9%

Source: Tsimpo and Wodon 2013b.

Table O.2 Private Cost of Schooling per Child for Households
US$ (average across the countries)

	Welfare quintiles					
	Q1	Q2	Q3	Q4	Q5	All
	Primary schools					
Public	4	5	6	9	18	7
Faith-inspired	8	14	17	28	54	26
Secular	16	27	39	50	144	84
Total	5	7	10	17	56	16
	Secondary schools					
Public	26	35	45	60	95	55
Faith-inspired	64	64	53	91	141	94
Private secular	39	58	105	104	227	168
Total	27	41	52	70	133	74

Source: Tsimpo and Wodon 2013b.

services provided to those groups, or relying on staffs who are willing to work at below market wages.

Summary statistics for the average costs by type of provider are provided in table O.2 and figure O.3 on the basis of data for eight of the 16 countries where that information was available. These are yearly costs in US dollars for primary and secondary schooling. These are not the total costs paid by households—for example transport costs are not included, nor are costs for uniforms and textbooks for examples, but these are the costs paid to schools for the services received. Apart from fees, PTA (Parent-Teacher Associations) dues are included, as these tend to fund operating expenses.

Finding #4: There are large differences in the private costs of education for households between providers, with faith-inspired schools costing more than public schools, but less than private secular schools.

Figure O.3 Average Private Cost of Schooling by Type of Provider
US$ (average across the countries)

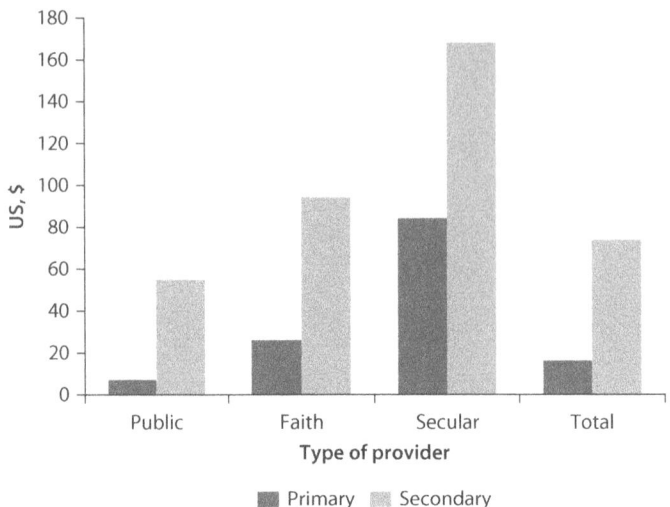

Source: Tsimpo and Wodon 2013b.

There is a clear ranking in costs between the various types of providers, with public schools being much cheaper, especially at the primary level where many countries have abolished most fees. Faith-inspired schools are more costly than public schools, but less costly than private secular schools. Costs are higher for those in the top quintiles as compared to lower quintiles, as expected, and it can also be shown that costs are higher in urban than in rural areas.

For example, table O.2 shows that the average cost of primary education is only US$7 in public schools, versus US$26 for faith-inspired schools and UD$84 for private secular schools. At the secondary level, the respective costs are US$55 in public schools, US$94 for faith-inspired schools, and UD$168 for private secular schools.

Satisfaction

In 7 of the 16 countries, data are available on satisfaction rates with the education services provided by various providers. Households are asked whether they have any complaints with the education received by children, and the absence of complaints is a measure of satisfaction.

The main results are provided in table O.3 and figure O.4. FISs enjoy higher satisfaction rates than public schools. For example, for the population as a whole, the satisfaction rate among FISs is on average 16 points higher for primary schools than in public schools, and 15 points higher for secondary schools. Private secular schools fare even slightly better, especially at the primary level. Satisfaction rates with faith-inspired schools tend however to be much lower in the bottom quintiles than in the top quintiles, suggesting a differentiation between various types of faith-inspired schools, some of which may be serving

Overview

Table O.3 Satisfaction Rates with the Various Types of Schools
percent (average across the countries)

	Welfare quintiles					
	Q1	Q2	Q3	Q4	Q5	All
	Primary schools					
Public	52	54	56	59	64	57
Faith-inspired	52	67	73	73	80	73
Secular	68	66	72	81	87	82
Total	53	56	59	63	72	61
	Secondary schools					
Public	60	60	60	59	63	61
Faith-inspired	47	61	76	72	80	76
Private secular	68	66	69	66	82	77
Total	60	60	62	61	69	64

Source: Tsimpo and Wodon 2013b.

Figure O.4 Satisfaction Rates with the Schooling Received
percent (average across the countries)

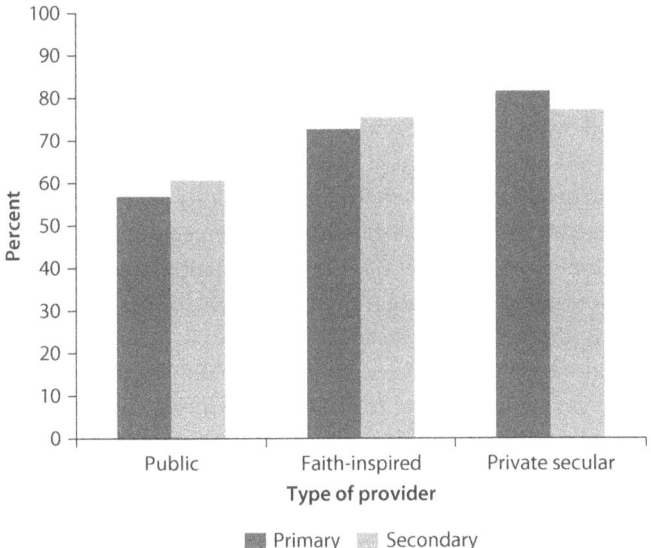

Source: Tsimpo and Wodon 2013b.

the very poor and others not (the gaps in satisfaction rates are smaller for public and private secular schools).

Finding #5: Private secular and faith-inspired schools have substantially higher satisfaction rates among parents than public schools.

What are the main reasons for nonsatisfaction? The questionnaires typically identify as potential reasons a lack of books/supplies, poor teaching, a lack of teachers, facilities in bad condition, overcrowding, a lack of furniture, and other problems. In a few countries, cost is also included as a potential reason for nonsatisfaction, but not in most. At the primary level, the lack of books and supplies is often the main reason for nonsatisfaction. Overcrowding and a lack of teachers are also mentioned, as well as many of the other problems. In secondary schools, the lack of books/supplies also comes first in most countries, but the lack of teachers comes up more often as a reason for nonsatisfaction.

It is important however to emphasize that the fact that the cost of schooling is not a major complaint in the statistics presented above does not mean that it is not an issue. The questions on satisfaction are asked to parents who have children in school—among parents who have children of school age not in school, it can be shown that cost is often the main, or at least a key reason for not being in school or dropping out.

Reasons for Choosing Specific Schools

Additional data were collected in two countries through focus groups and in-depth interviews to better understand the reasons why some parents chose to send their children to faith-inspired schools (see box O.2 for the methodology).

Box O.2 Data Sources—Qualitative Work

Qualitative data were collected by the World Bank between April and June 2010 in Ghana and Burkina Faso. These data were collected through interviews with parents, head teachers, and school principals for a total of eight or nine schools per country in one urban and one rural location in each of the two countries. The schools were selected with inputs from district education officials, but the main criterion was the requirement that there should be both public and faith-inspired schools in the areas where the qualitative work was conducted. The areas had to have both Christian and Islamic schools apart from public schools.

A semi-structured questionnaire was used to interview individuals sending their children to the schools. Each interview took from one hour to one hour and a half, and focused in large part on the perceptions of the schools and the reasons that led individuals to choose one school versus another. Both responses to open-ended questions and closed questions will be used in the analysis. In the case of closed questions, quantitative statistics were estimated in percentage terms from those interviews, but it must be emphasized that the sample is small in both countries. A separate semi-structured questionnaire was also administered to the school principals and administrators as well as to a few teachers. A few additional interviews were conducted with key informants, such as officials from the Ministries of Education.

In Ghana among those sending their children to Christian schools, faith is a key motivation for half (50.0 percent) of the parents (see table O.4). The share is even higher at 75.0 percent for parents sending their children to Islamic schools (37.5 percent of parents in Islamic schools also mentioned that learning Arabic was important). In addition to the role of faith and values, quality also mattered,

Table O.4 Main Reasons for Choosing the School, Qualitative Field Work, 2010
percent

	Islamic schools	Christian schools	Secular schools
		Ghana	
Location	20.8	16.7	37.5
Religion	75.0	50.0	6.3
Morals, values	—	29.2	—
Learn Arabic	37.5	—	—
Learn English	4.2	—	—
Teacher quality	4.2	33.3	25.0
Academics	4.2	16.7	25.0
Future schooling/job	4.2	4.2	—
Know the school	16.7	16.7	18.8
Low or no fees	4.2	—	31.3
Low cost books	4.2	—	—
Curriculum	29.2	4.2	—
		Burkina Faso	
Location	38.7	33.3	70.0
Religion	83.9	33.3	—
Morals, values	35.5	36.7	—
Learn Arabic	29.0	—	—
Learn French	25.8	—	3.3
Teacher quality	12.9	46.7	10.0
Academics	25.8	76.7	46.7
Future schooling/job	9.7	6.7	16.7
Know the school	—	6.7	13.3
Low or no fees	—	—	30.0
No proselytizing	—	—	16.7

Sources: Shojo and Wodon 2013; Gemignani and Wodon 2013.
Note: Multiple answers allowed. — = not available.

especially for parents relying on Christian schools. For some of these parents, quality issues did lead to a change in school for their children.

Finding #6: Faith and values are key reasons why some parents chose faith-inspired schools, with quality also playing a role especially for the choice of Christian schools.

Similar results were obtained in Burkina Faso where parents at Christian schools said that they chose their school for its academic and teacher quality (76.7 percent and 46.7 percent, respectively). By contrast, respondents in Islamic schools more often said that their choice of school was largely based on the opportunity for their children to receive a religious education (83.9 percent), with smaller numbers listing academic or teacher quality (25.8 percent and 12.9 percent respectively). In public schools, location was a deciding factor for 70 percent of parents, followed by academic quality (46.7 percent) and the lack of school fees (30.0 percent).

Education on moral values was listed as a reason for school choice by about a third of parents in Islamic and Christian schools, but by no parents in public schools (see box O.3 for examples of brief testimonies by parents in FISs).

Box O.3 Example of Testimonies by Parents

"The school is strict and disciplines the children. Apart from academic subjects, Christian values are instilled in the children, and that makes them obedient." (Parent at a public Christian school)

"When the children complete this type of school, they will be knowledgeable in both academic subjects and Islamic studies." (Parent at a private Islamic school)

The importance of religion also emerges from comments made by parents: "Because this school is an Islamic school, they teach Arabic and English. That is why I prefer this school to secular schools" (Parent at a public Islamic school); "Children in the other schools are not as disciplined like the children here. The fear of the Lord is taught and also the church supports us. I want my children to be brought up in the Christian faith" (Parent at a private Christian school).

Another question was asked about the advantages of the school chosen by parents. In both countries faith and values came again strongly as key advantages among those sending their children to Christian and Islamic schools. Overall, faith clearly matters for the choice of a faith-inspired school, and this appears to be especially the case for Islamic schools.

Performance

The study also reports on a few measures of comparative performance, again with a focus on Ghana and Burkina Faso. The data are however weaker, so conclusions are tentative. In both countries, students appear to do slightly better in private schools than in public schools. In Ghana for example, 65 percent of students in public schools can read in English, and 59 percent can write in English. The corresponding shares in faith-inspired schools are 71 percent and 63 percent, and they are even higher in private secular schools at 89 percent and 83 percent. Similarly, the share of students who can do a written calculation is lower in public schools, at 90 percent, than in faith-inspired and private secular schools, at 92 percent and 96 percent respectively. Within faith-inspired schools, some differences are also observed. In the Burkina Faso for example, students in Christian schools tend to do better than students in Islamic schools. Yet all these results need to be interpreted with caution. In the case of Ghana, when relying on regression analysis, students in private secular schools continue to do better than students in public schools, but this is not the case anymore for students in faith-inspired school, especially in rural areas.

Finding #7: There is tentative evidence that students in faith-inspired schools, and especially those in private secular schools, perform better than students in public schools, but more research is needed in this area.

Conclusion

Despite the important role of faith-inspired and private secular schools in education service delivery in Africa, limited systematic evidence is available today on their market share, reach to the poor, cost, and satisfaction among users, in comparison with public schools. This study aimed to close some of that knowledge gap. Six main findings emerge from the analysis:

1. The average market share for faith-inspired schools is 10–15 percent, and that for private secular schools is of a similar order of magnitude.
2. On average, faith-inspired schools do not reach the poor more than other groups; they also do not reach the poor more than public schools, but they do reach the poor significantly more than private secular schools.
3. The cost for households of faith-inspired schools is higher than that of public schools, possibly because of lack of public funding, but lower than that of private secular schools.
4. Faith-inspired and private secular schools have higher satisfaction rates among parents than public schools.
5. Parents using faith-inspired schools place a strong emphasis on religious education and moral values.
6. Students in faith-inspired and private schools perform better than those in public schools, but this may be due in part to self-selection.

This study was devoted to a basic diagnostic of the role of private schools in education in Africa. What are some of the important areas for further research?

A first priority is to conduct research on how to deal with the risk of duplication of efforts and the lack of harmonization between education providers. To minimize such risks, detailed pictures of the service delivery landscape at both the local and national levels are needed. It is also important to promote more public-private partnerships between FISs and governments.

A second priority is to better understand the constraints in private schools, and especially the faith-inspired schools that serve the poor operate, the challenges they face, and the opportunities they offer. How can faith-inspired schools serve the poor when the sources of revenues available to them are limited, which raises cost recovery from households? How can these schools maintain their distinctive vision and culture while being progressively more integrated into national education systems? How can the capacity of the schools to evaluate their interventions, as well as to assess the extent to which they reach the poor, be expanded?

A third sets of questions, not discussed in this study, relates to the impact of faith on behaviors, not only as it relates to the choice of service provider, but also more generally. In many areas such as child marriage, which has implications for education outcomes, faith-related practices and cultural traditions play an important role, underscoring the potential of engaging religious and traditional leaders as well as faith-inspired schools in efforts to eradicate such practices.

Given that the market share of FISs may be smaller than many had thought, and that their reach to the poor is also limited even if their contribution should not be understated, it could very well be that one of the more important roles that faith and values play in education is related to their impact on a wide range of behaviors, and not only service delivery. Questions related to faith and behaviors that affect education and other human development outcomes are often more difficult to understand, and also more difficult to influence through government policies than issues related directly to service delivery, but certainly not less important to consider.

In addition, better understanding of why many faith-inspired schools seem to provide a good-quality education despite limited budgets could also be beneficial for advancing the "learning for all" agenda.

CHAPTER 1

Introduction

Within the context of Millennium Development Goals (MDGs), donors and governments in developing countries have made improvements in human development a key priority. Public sector service providers continue to have a leading role in efforts to improve education outcomes, but private providers, including faith-inspired schools (FISs), may also contribute. Given that many developing countries may miss the education targets of the MDGs, it is all the more important for donors as well as national and local governments to recognize the role played by FISs, and where appropriate to support them in their service delivery activities, especially when they reach the poor. Unfortunately, empirical assessments of the role that FISs have played or could play in improving education outcomes and providing services have not been conducted to-date. Such assessments are especially needed at the national and local levels where development policies and interventions are negotiated and implemented.

Both the supply and demand sides of service delivery in education deserve attention. First, on the supply side of service delivery, it is often argued that FISs provide a large share of education services, especially in Sub-Saharan Africa, and that their services are better targeted to the poor, more cost effective, and of higher quality than those of other providers. These assertions, if correct, could have major implications for policy, since governments (as well as donors) would then be more inclined to support FISs in their activities. Unfortunately, the evidence to back up such statements remains rather limited and is often contentious.

Second, on the demand side of service delivery, it is often argued that faith plays an important role in decisions made by individuals and households about education. Examples include whether parents send girls to school and the types of schools chosen. In this study, the focus is on the satisfaction of the users of the services provided by FISs, and why parents choose to use faith-inspired, other private, or public facilities for their education needs. Again the data are limited—or not yet properly analyzed and interpreted—on the satisfaction of households with the services provided by various providers, and on the preferences that affect the choice of providers by households. For example, is faith a key factor in the choice of service provider, and is the importance of preferences related to faith similar for Muslims and Christians? Because of limited analysis on those issues, faith and more generally values are typically not (specifically) taken into account when designing development interventions.

The purpose of the study is to provide an empirical assessment of the role that FISs play in the supply of Education services in Sub-Saharan Africa, with more detailed work conducted for Ghana and Burkina Faso. In what follows, the next two chapters are meant to provide background for the rest of the study. Chapter 2 provides information on the conceptual framework that informs the study. Chapter 3 describes the methodology and data used for the study, with a focus on nationally representative household surveys that provide new evidence on the market share, reach to the poor, cost, and performance of FISs in comparison with other service providers. The methodology for the collection of additional data, including qualitative fieldwork conducted in Ghana and Burkina Faso, is also described.

The next three chapters are devoted to an assessment of the market share and reach to the poor of FISs, as well as their cost for households. Chapter 4 deals with the market share debate. It is often claimed that FISs account for 40 percent or more of service provision in African countries, but the evidence on which such claims are based is thin. The chapter presents new sets of estimates of the role of FISs based on national household surveys.

Next, chapter 5 looks at whether FISs reach the poor in priority when providing services, and at whether they make special efforts to do so. Once again the perception that FISs reach the poor in priority is not necessarily confirmed by the data from household surveys. On average FISs are not serving the poor more in absolute terms, nor are they serving the poor proportionately more than public facilities, even if they often appear to make special efforts to do so. They do, on the other hand, serve the poor substantially more than secular private providers, and many FISs appear to make efforts to reach the poor and other vulnerable groups.

Chapter 6 considers the cost of the education services provided by FISs. In the absence of support from the state, or in cases where lower levels of support are received by FISs than by public facilities, the need for FISs to achieve cost recovery may make their services less affordable for the poor. At the same time, FISs may be able to tap into other sources of funding, especially from congregations and other religious groups nationally or abroad. Chapter 6 relies on various sources of data to assess the private cost of education for households.

The last chapter is more focused on the demand for the services provided by FISs. It looks at the satisfaction of users with various types of facilities and the reasons why some individual and households use the services provided by FISs. Limited analysis is also conducted on the performance of FISs. The analysis suggests that FISs tend to provide services of better quality than public providers, at least as measured through satisfaction rates among users, with the higher level of satisfaction with FISs related in part to better service and the fact that FISs do place an emphasis on religion and values in the education provided to children.

As to good data on performance for FISs, it is hard to come by. But subjective assessments of literacy and numeracy are available in the household surveys and can thus be used. The evidence does not suggest that students in faith-inspired schools as a whole do better than students in public schools, while students in private secular schools appear to be doing slightly better, but this specific evidence is provided for only one country, so that is should not be generalized.

Overall, it is hoped that the study provides the first comprehensive empirical analysis of the role that FISs play in efforts towards providing education services in Sub-Saharan Africa, with more details for the cases studies devoted to Ghana and Burkina Faso. It is also hoped that the analysis is innovative by relying on both nationally representative household surveys that have not yet been used for this purpose and qualitative fieldwork. It is finally hoped that the study will be of interest to a wide range of readers, including the staff of FISs, policy makers, and development practitioners working for local and national governments as well as donors and all those who are interested in what is often referred to as "faith in action."

CHAPTER 2

Motivation and Background

Introduction

This study aims to contribute to better empirical evidence and knowledge about the contribution of faith-inspired schools (FISs) to service delivery in education in Sub-Saharan Africa, with additional work for two country studies in Ghana and Burkina Faso. Part of the debate about the role of FISs in service delivery has been framed within the broader discussion on markets and public-private partnerships, at least in the economics literature. As noted by Barrera-Osorio et al. (2009b), part of this literature compares the performance of private and public schools. Even if this is not always the case, there is some evidence that private schools, including faith-inspired schools, may provide better services and achieve better education outcomes than public schools (on this topic, see among others Allcott and Ortega 2009; Altonji et al. 2005; Asadullah et al. 2009; Cox and Jimenez 1990; Evans and Schwab 1995; González and Arévalo 2005; Hoxby 1994; Hsieh and Urquiola 2006; Wodon and Ying 2009; Parra Osorio and Wodon 2011).

Another strand in the literature focuses on the reasons that could explain the gains often associated with private schools, including faith-inspired schools (Epple and Romano 1998; LaRocque and Patrinos 2006; Nechyba 2000; Savas 2000). First, private schools may introduce competition in the education sector and thereby raise overall quality. Second, private providers may have more flexibility than public providers in the management of the schools. Third, to the extent that private providers of education are competitively selected, better providers would emerge in the private as opposed to the public sphere. Fourth, risk-sharing between the government and the private sector may also lead to better overall provision.

Yet much of the evidence on the quality of faith-inspired schools has been obtained from high- (and sometimes middle-) income countries, and many of the arguments about the benefits of private provision in education have been made principally in the context of developed countries. While these arguments also hold to some extent for developing countries, some differences must be pointed out. First, in many countries in Africa, especially in rural areas where the majority of the population still lives, many households may not have many choices with regards to where to send their children to school, so that competition and risk sharing are likely to be more limited than in developed countries. Education provision in those areas is also often not profitable, so that there are limited incentives for competitive selection between private providers, even though some competition does take place. Finally, many FISs tend to rely at least in part on public funding, which also implies that flexibility may be limited, for example for the design of the curriculum that is taught, or in the ability of faith-inspired schools to hire and fire teachers.

This suggests that the benefits from the contribution of private and faith-inspired schools identified in the economics literature—such as competition, flexibility, selection, and risk-sharing—may perhaps not materialize as much in poor African countries as they may in developed countries. The potential benefits from faith-inspired schools for students may instead come more from the special dedication to their mission that these providers often have.

Still, this does not mean that the basic insights from the economics literature, and what is often referred to as rational choice theory in the religious studies literature (see appendix A) —namely that individuals practice their faith in various areas of their life taking into account the benefits and costs of doing so—do not apply when discussing the supply of education services by FISs, or the demand for such services by households. These services are provided in a market that is often at least somewhat competitive, with different schools facilities accessible to households. At the local level, where there is a faith-inspired facility, there is often also a public facility nearby, and (less often) a private secular facility. Individuals are often willing to travel some distance to attend a certain school when the school is perceived to provide services of higher quality. This means that even if in a given village, there may be only one school, competition may be there through another facility located in a nearby village.

Furthermore, as shown in chapter 5 and contrary to popular belief, most FISs do not necessarily serve mostly the poor in remote rural areas. Backiny-Yetna and Wodon (2009a) suggest for example that in Cameroon, faith-inspired schools tend to cater to a relatively well-off and mostly urban clientele. What adds to competitive pressures at the local level is the fact that education services are consumed for a price—even if special efforts are made by FISs to make their services affordable, and in some cases even free, for the poor. Significant cost recovery is often requested from clients by service providers through various types of fees, and this takes place whether one considers public, faith-inspired, or private secular providers. In geographic areas where different types of providers are present, price differentiation between providers is observed, which affects where households choose to put their children in school.

Competition between providers is based in part on prices, but also on quality and perceptions of quality. As already mentioned, it is often argued that FISs provide services of better quality than the public sector, and this study will provide some empirical evidence to that effect. At the same time, FISs may perhaps not provide the best services available, simply because of the financial constraints they face. When FISs aim to serve the poor, they tend not to charge as much as private secular providers. Higher levels of cost recovery from users then gives an advantage to private secular providers in providing education services that may be of higher quality than those provided by FISs, and thereby in achieving higher performance.

Mentioning that FISs provide services in a market place that is competitive with competition taking place among others through prices and quality, so that FISs must take into account the various costs and benefits of the options available to them, is stating the obvious. Does this mean that on the supply side faith plays no role in what FISs chose to do? Or that on the demand side faith does not matter in individual decisions related to education? Not at all: faith does matters, whether one considers the supply of services (faith motivates many of those who work for FISs and the decisions made by FIS managers) or the demand for services (faith influences those using the services provided).

On the supply side, faith is often at the core of the *ethos* of FISs and their workers, which can lead FISs to behave differently from other (especially for-profit) providers. An example of this is provided by Reinikka and Svensson (2010) in their work on Uganda. The authors use a change in financing of not-for-profit healthcare providers through untied government grants to test two theories of organizational behavior. The first theory postulates that not-for-profit providers are intrinsically motivated to serve the poor and will therefore use new resources to expand their services or cut the cost of these services. The second theory postulates that not-for-profit providers are captured by their managers or workers and behave like for-profit actors. Although they may not appropriate profits, they would tend to use untied grants to raise the salaries of their staff or provide them with other benefits that would not directly serve the poor. The authors' empirical results suggest that the first altruistic theory is validated by the data, and that the results matter in the sense that this altruistic behavior makes a difference for the poor.

On the demand side as well, faith may play an important, and in some cases decisive, role, given the importance of faith in many people's lives in the developing world (Tsimpo and Wodon 2013a). A few examples help in illustrating how this may happen. First, faith may influence the choice of service provider by individuals and households. One of the findings of this study is that faith does play a key role for at least part of the population when choosing an education provider. This is because the values taught at school—and in the case of Muslims the inclusion of Islamic studies in the curriculum—are very important for some parents. As a second example, consider the role that faith plays in behaviors that in turn affect the demand for service delivery. If within a specific faith tradition, girls do not tend to go to school after a certain age, say in part because of early marriages, this then affects the demand for schooling in that tradition. Because faith does matter in many people's life, it does influence the choices made by individuals and households, which in turn may have direct or indirect implications for service delivery.

In terms of conceptual framework on those issues, a standard reference for a synthesis of recent research on service delivery in developing countries, especially for the poor, is the World Development Report entitled *Making Services Work for Poor People* (World Bank 2004). The framework used in that report focuses on four sets of actors: citizens/clients who use services, politicians and policy makers who regulate national service delivery systems and manage networks of public providers, organizational providers—the public and private entities or facilities that provide services, and, finally, frontline professionals such as teachers who deliver the services. The emphasis throughout the report is on accountability, defined as a relationship among two or more sets of actors that has five main features, namely delegation, finance, performance, information about performance, and enforceability.

Today much of the research on service delivery is focused on how to make accountability relationships work, so that better services are provided at an affordable cost to the poor. For example, which incentives work best for teachers to actually show up in class? Or what are the features of successful public-private partnerships and contractual arrangements for the delivery of services? In economics and more generally in the realm of program evaluation, much of the research on service delivery is rather sophisticated. Randomization is often considered as the gold standard for assessing the impact of any given intervention or program, and when this is not feasible, complex econometric methodologies are used to tease out impacts. This level of sophistication is in part the result of the fact that many of the more basic questions, in terms of measuring access to services, targeting to the poor, cost, and performance have been answered, at least as they pertain to public service delivery.

In this study, some of the sections will rely on econometric or experimental techniques, but most of the analysis will not, simply because many of the basic questions on the role of FISs in service delivery still have not been answered. This study will provide econometric results when appropriate. But because most of the work conducted on service delivery has not considered the role of faith explicitly, the study will often give substantial space to establishing basic stylized facts, as opposed to conducting more advanced research on specific program interventions or alternative accountability mechanisms. It is hoped that by establishing basic stylized facts more firmly, and by showing that there are data available to conduct some of the more sophisticated work, the study will encourage others to follow suit.

Comparative Advantage of Faith-Inspired Institutions

The purpose of this study is to assess empirically whether what is often said about the market share, reach to the poor, cost, and quality of FISs in service delivery in Africa is actually correct. A key aspect of what is said about FISs is that they may have a comparative advantage in the delivery of certain services, but that they may also suffer from comparative disadvantages in other areas. Such comparative advantages and weaknesses are important, given that individuals and households choose their service providers depending on a range of factors, including costs, quality, and faith-specific considerations. As to the administrators and staff of FISs, they also consider various factors—including their perceived comparative advantages and weaknesses—in making decisions about the range and types of services that they should provide. These decisions by both households and by FISs should then in turn be taken into account by governments and line ministries when considering various education policies or programs.

In this broad context, there are at least two ways of thinking of the comparative advantage of FISs. A first approach consists in considering the faith orientation of FISs as a specific comparative advantage in and of itself, at least towards some segments of the population. For example, models can be constructed, and hypotheses can be tested, to assess whether households who tend to be more religious favor specific types of schools, so that their children receive a specific type of education. An illustration of such models is presented in appendix A based on a paper by Cohen-Zada and Sander (2008).

Another way to think of the potential comparative advantages and disadvantages of FISs is to look at secular attributes of service delivery, and to compare FISs to other providers along those attributes. With specific reference to healthcare services in Sub-Saharan Africa, Lipsky (2011) provides a review of the literature on such comparative advantages of FISs as compared to nongovernmental organizations (NGOs) (for a broader review of the literature on religion and development, see Deneulin and Rakodi (2011)).[1] While this is not the only such review of the literature, and while it focuses on healthcare as opposed to education, it is handy in the way that it synthesizes much of the evidence to-date, and it is likely that much of what Lipsky attributes as specific characteristics of FISs or NGOs in the case of healthcare services could also be attributed to similar organizations involved in education services. In order to make more precise what is done in this study and what is not done in comparison to the literature, and in order to compare some of the results of this study with the literature, it is useful to review Lipsky's findings and those of this study.

Table 2.1 provides the list of strengths and weaknesses identified by Lipsky for FISs and NGOs. The table also provides a brief assessment of the findings of this study, where the comparison is not between FISs and NGOs, but between FISs, public providers, and private secular providers, most of which are for-profit. The ratings provided for FISs and NGOs in the first two columns are those given by Lipsky, and the ratings in the next three columns are based on this study. The top rating is a "3," which suggests that FISs or NGOs are very likely to have a comparative advantage (or a weakness) in any given area. A rating of "2" suggests that FISs or NGOs are likely to benefit from a comparative advantage. A rating of "1" suggests a lower but still positive likelihood of this being the case. A rating of "0" suggests no comparative advantage (or no weakness in an area). The symbol "—" suggests that a specific aspect is not analyzed in the review by Lipsky or in this study. In a nutshell, table 2.1 provides an overview of what the literature says about the comparative advantage of FISs, and what is found in this study.

At least three points can be made about table 2.1. First, in terms of scope, there are differences in the topics considered in the broader literature on service delivery by FISs and those covered here. Here the focus is on a few specific aspects of service delivery—namely the assessment of the market share,

Table 2.1 Potential Comparative Advantages and Weaknesses of FISs

	Lipsky		This study		
	NGOs	FISs	FISs	Public	Private secular
			Comparative advantage		
Service delivery					
Market share	—	—	1	3	2
Reach to the poor	—	—	2	2	1
Low cost of services for the poor	—	—	2	3	1
Deliver quality services	1	1	2	1	3
Differentiated service provision	—	—	3	1	2
Organizational traits					
Moral and ethical standing	1	2	3	1	—
Understanding of local context	1	3	2	2	—
Increased flexibility	1	3	—	—	—
Increased transparency and accountability	1	0	—	—	—
Beneficiary empowerment					
Build constituency	1	1	—	—	—
Help communities form their own representative bodies	1	0	—	—	—
Connect local communities with higher authorities	1	0	—	—	—
Foster joint learning	1	1	—	—	—
Other roles					
Speaks on behalf of disenfranchised	1	1	—	—	—
Mobilize energy and resources	1	3	1	2	2
Provide feedback to donors and government	1	0	2	3	1
Contribute to consensus building	1	1	—	—	—
			Comparative weaknesses		
Amateurism	1	2	1	1	1
Particularism	1	2	1	1	1
Paternalism	1	2	—	—	—
Insufficiency	1	1	—	—	—

Source: Adapted and expanded from Lipsky 2011.
Note: In Lipsky, symbols are used instead of ratings of 0–3, but the message is the same. A higher value implies a higher likelihood of having a comparative advantage or weakness. NGOs = nongovernmental organizations; FISs = faith-inspired schools; — = not available.

reach to the poor, cost and funding, and user satisfaction rates of FISs, as well as the reasons why households choose FISs. The treatment of many of those topics is hopefully more thorough in this study than in the existing literature, and this is the contribution of the study. Yet one should be aware that the broader literature considers other issues, such as the organizational traits of FISs, the extent to which they succeed in empowering their beneficiaries, and some other roles they may play which are only briefly discussed here. While some of the findings in this study have relevance for some of these other questions, such as the moral and ethical standing of FISs, their understanding of the local context, or their dialogue with government, the scope of this study is necessarily limited, with many interesting questions not debated, or at least not discussed in-depth.

Second, in terms of findings on comparative advantages, Lipsky suggests that the main comparative advantage of FISs is their moral and ethical standing with local populations, which helps in raising funds, recruiting staffs and volunteers, and understanding the local context, and in turn leads to flexibility in the way they operate. It is unclear on the other hand whether FISs are better than NGOs in other areas, such as speaking on behalf of the disenfranchised, contributing to consensus building and connecting communities with higher authorities, or delivering quality services. This study suggests similar findings, but also with some differences.

In terms of areas not covered by Lipsky in detail, this study suggests that FISs have a smaller market share than is often believed, that they reach the poor about to the same extent as the public sector does, and that they tend to be more expensive for households. In comparison to private secular providers, FISs do reach the poor more and at lower cost. In terms of common areas of focus, one apparent difference between Lipsky's conclusions and this study's findings relates to the quality of the services provided. Lipsky rates both FISs and NGOs as having only a somewhat likely comparative advantage in that area. While recognizing heterogeneity in the quality of services provided by different FISs, this study suggests a strong comparative advantage for FISs, at least as measured through user satisfaction among FISs and the reasons for choosing those facilities. For education the fact that faith-inspired schools give a larger place to faith and values is appreciated by parents relying on their services (this is why the area of "differentiation" was added in table 2.1). It could be that the moral and ethical standing of FISs is indeed at the source of these differences in user satisfaction. Clearly this is a key comparative advantage for schools when parents care about values. But it may also be that higher user satisfaction with FISs is related to a tradition of service that is not directly the result of the FISs' moral and ethical standing. While this study will not venture into what exactly is the reason for the higher level of satisfaction among users of FISs, it does suggest a comparative advantage there.

Third, in terms of potential weaknesses, Lipsky suggests that FISs may be more at risk of amateurism, particularism, and paternalism than NGOs, that they may be less transparent and accountable than NGOs, and that they have fewer interactions with donors and governments. In this study there is little evidence of amateurism, particularism (in terms of relying on religion to select those who are served, or in terms of whether FISs proselytize), and paternalism on the part of FISs, and the FISs that are being reviewed appear to be relatively transparent and accountable. Many are also interacting with governments. This difference in findings may be related in part to differences in focus between Lipsky's review and this study. While Lipsky considers a wider set of FISs, this study focuses on school-based providers.

Now, one should not try to infer too much from table 2.1 because it only provides a very broad brush summary of some of the findings in Lipsky's review of the literature and in this study. But the table hopefully helps to locate what this study focuses on within the literature on FISs in Sub-Saharan Africa, and in showing how differences in assessments can be made depending on the evidence at hand and the set of comparators used.

Combination of Cross-Country and Country-Specific Work

This study considers Sub-Saharan Africa as a whole, but additional work is done on two countries—Ghana and Burkina Faso. The basic idea is that looking in more details at a few case studies helps in better understanding the role that FISs have in service delivery in a specific country context, beyond the provision of statistics for Africa as a whole, or at least the countries where the analysis can be conducted. Why were Ghana and Burkina Faso chosen for the more detailed work? The reasons for this choice were both strategic and opportunistic.

From a strategic point of view, three main reasons led to the choice of Ghana and Burkina Faso as case studies. The first reason is the fact that both countries are religiously diverse, with Christian, Muslim, and traditionalist populations. While Ghana is a majority Christian country, Burkina Faso is a majority Muslim country. Looking at two religiously diverse countries allows for potentially interesting comparisons between faith traditions. On the supply side of service delivery, is the role of Christian and Muslim FISs different, both in terms of the scope of their activities and their characteristics? On the demand side, is the impact of faith on the demand for services by FISs different for Christian and Muslim populations? While for most of this study, the data do not permit an exploration of diversity within the Christian and Muslim traditions, comparisons between these two traditions do reveal interesting differences.

The second reason behind the choice of Ghana and Burkina Faso is that it also provides for interesting comparisons between societies that have had different colonial experiences. Ghana was a British colony, and Burkina Faso a French one. Besides differences in language and culture, these colonial histories may have contributed to differences in the role that FISs play in health and education systems today. The French model of state governance, which tends to be centralized, led in former colonies to the creation of strong public delivery systems for education (and healthcare), which left less space for private service delivery, including by FISs. By contrast, under the more decentralized British system, FISs were able to expand more easily, which led in some cases to more significant market shares. Considering both one English- and one French-speaking country in this study thus helps to have a more balanced view of the role of FISs in service delivery in Sub-Saharan Africa, given heterogeneity in such roles between countries.

Finally, Ghana and Burkina Faso are at different stages of their development, which is the third strategic reason that led to the choice of these two countries for the study. Ghana has made great progress towards many of the Millennium Development Goal (MDGs), including by reducing the share of its population in poverty by almost half between the early 1990s and 2005/06 (Coulombe and Wodon 2007). Progress towards poverty reduction has also been accomplished in Burkina Faso, but not as rapidly (Nouve et al. 2009, 2010).Education outcomes are also better in Ghana than in Burkina Faso. In terms of levels of gross domestic product (GDP) per capita, while Ghana recently reached the lower-middle-income status, Burkina Faso is still a low-income country. World Bank estimates suggest a GDP per capita in Ghana of US$1190 under the Atlas method in 2009, while the corresponding figure for Burkina Faso is US$510 (the difference in PPP-adjusted GDP per capita is smaller).

Diversity in faiths within each country, as well as diversity between the two countries in colonial experience, the role of FISs, and levels of development are the strategic reasons that led to the choice of Ghana and Burkina Faso as focus countries for this study. But there were also opportunistic reasons for this choice of countries, in terms of the availability of data. Indeed, as mentioned in chapter 3, substantial data are available on both countries, and especially in Ghana, in terms of individual or household surveys.

Conclusion

There has been a renewed interest in the role of faith and FISs in development among policy practitioners. The recognition that faith may affect development in multiple ways has led leading agencies such as the United Nations to step up their work in this area. Yet as these organizations are paying more attention to the so-called faith sector, it has also become evident that the evidence base on which policy makers could rely to guide their engagement with that sector remains weak. For example, existing estimates of the market share of FISs in service delivery in Africa are poorly documented, and may be higher than warranted. The objective of this study is to contribute a small step towards filling this empirical evidence and knowledge gap for Sub-Saharan Africa, with more detailed work for Ghana and Burkina Faso.

Note

1. Lipsky (2011) uses the term faith-based organization (FBO) instead of FIS, but this does not matter much for the purpose of this study. On terminology, see the discussion in chapter 2.

CHAPTER 3

Data and Methodology

Introduction

This chapter provides background information on the methodology and data used for this study. Pretty much the same approach is used in each of the chapters that follows, so that it is useful to start by describing what that approach or structure is. Essentially, the chapters start with an introduction that lays out the question at hand. Next, the second section of each chapter, typically entitled "cross-country evidence," provides comparative information for up to 16 Sub-Saharan countries on the topic discussed in the chapter. Given that many issues or findings are country- and context-specific, the next section then provides additional evidence on the two countries selected for more in-depth case studies, namely Ghana and Burkina Faso. The material in that section tends to be different in each chapter, because it depends on the type of additional evidence that has been collected and analyzed—sometimes the additional evidence may be quantitative, sometimes it may be qualitative, and sometimes it may be combined. In some cases additional evidence is available for both Ghana and Burkina Faso, but in other cases the additional evidence may be available only for one country. In several cases, because of data availability, more additional evidence is available for Ghana than for Burkina Faso.

This general structure for the chapters that follow guides the way in which the sections on data and methodology in this chapter are organized, with section 2 devoted to a brief discussion of the national surveys used for many countries (see also appendix C), and section 3 discussing more detailed qualitative data sources of data for Ghana and Burkina Faso. Beyond information on data sources, this chapter also discusses a few methodological issues that warrant attention. First, in section 4, questions are asked about the validity of the data at hand for the purpose of the study, as well as the techniques that are used for statistical and econometric work conducted with the surveys. For example, a first question is whether there is a serious risk of misidentification of faith-inspired schools (FISs) in the survey, and if so, what might be the consequences of such misidentification. Another question is how the poor are defined using the various household surveys, given that there are differences between various surveys on how this is done. More importantly, when comparing the cost of various providers for households, or their performance and the satisfaction of users, it is useful to estimate econometric models that control for a range of household and possibly individual characteristics. How this is done while acknowledging the fact that the choice of the type of provider used itself depends on the same characteristics (the endogeneity issue) is also discussed in section 4.

Finally, section 5 emphasizes two limits in the scope of the study. Firstly, the study focuses on service delivery, as opposed to the broader set of issues related to faith and human development. Secondly, the study focuses for the most part on facilities-based services—that is, the services provided by schools, hospitals and clinics. This is related to a broader debate about what is meant by a FIS. The debate on the most appropriate term to be used—such as FIS, faith-based organization (FBO), or other terms—is essentially brushed aside in this study, except when a discussion of terms is needed for the question at hand. Given the limits of the data being used, it is enough here to associate FISs to faith-inspired physical facilities that provide education services. Without evidence in the household surveys on the role of other types of FISs, there is no need to enter into a debate on the terminology used in the literature to distinguish between various types of FISs. Thus, the lack of discussion of terminology should not be construed as a statement that terminology does not matter. The many terms used in the literature point to a complex reality on the ground and a high degree of heterogeneity among FISs. But for this study, that debate on terminology and the many types of FISs matters less.

Household Survey Data

This study relies on both nationally representative household surveys and qualitative fieldwork data—the reason for doing so is detailed in appendix. Consider first nationally representative household survey data. To-date, such surveys in which households are asked about the type of education facility they use when seeking care or providing an education for their children have not been drawn much into the discussion about the role of FISs in Africa. This is due in part to the fact that the surveys most frequently used for comparative work on human development, the Demographic and Health Surveys (DHS), do not permit the identification of faith-inspired facilities separately from the other facilities used by households. The advantage of the DHS is that the surveys typically have the same questions, or at least very similar questions, asked in different countries. The surveys also are available after a short lag on a publicly accessible website. This makes conducting comparative empirical work across countries easier. Unfortunately, in the case of education, the standard questionnaire does not separate public and private facilities when asking where children are going to school.

For this study, instead of using DHS data, the analysis is based on multipurpose and nationally representative household surveys implemented in 16 African countries (see table 3.1; the 16 counties were selected from a larger pool for

Table 3.1 Identification of FISs in the Education Modules of Selected Household Surveys

Country	Identification in the survey of FISs for education
Benin (QUIBB 2003)	No
Burkina Faso (EACVM-QUIBB 2007)	Yes
Burundi (QUIBB 2006)	Yes
Cameroon (ECAM 2007)	Yes
Cape Verde (QUIBB 2007)	No
Chad (ECOSIT2 2003/04)	No
Cote d'Ivoire (ENV 2002)	No
Democratic Republic of Congo (123 survey 2004/05)	Yes
Gabon (EGEP-QUIBB 2005)	No
Ghana (CWIQ 2003)	Yes
Ghana (GLSS5 2005/06)	Yes
Guinea (ELEP-QUIBB 2007)	No
Kenya (KIHBS 2005)	Yes
Liberia (CWIQ 2007)	No
Malawi (HIS-2 2004)	Yes
Mali (ELIM-QUIBB 2006)	Yes
Niger (ENBC 2007)	Yes
Nigeria (LMS 2003/04)	Yes
ROC (ECOM-QUIBB 2005)	Yes
Rwanda (EICV 2001)	No
Senegal (ESPS 2005)	Yes
Sierra Leone (SLIHS 2003)	Yes
Swaziland (SHIES 2009)	Yes
Togo (QUIBB 2006)	No
Uganda (UNHS 2010)	Yes
Zambia (LCMS IV 2004)	Yes
Number of countries with identification	16

Source: Compiled by World Bank. See appendix C for more details on the surveys with identification.
Note: FISs = faith-inspired schools.

which data were available). The choice of the countries was in part opportunistic, in terms of the accessibility of the unit level data to the author. But it was also purposeful, in the sense that special efforts were made to have a broadly representative set of countries, including some of the larger ones such as Nigeria or the Democratic Republic of Congo. These multipurpose surveys are the surveys that are typically used for poverty measurement, as well as for preparing broader socioeconomic profiles, among others. But these surveys also have detailed education modules, which are used here.

The education modules of the surveys typically ask whether children go to school, at what level, and in which type of school. Information is also sometimes available on the cost of education for households or individual household members, as well as on the satisfaction with the education received, and the reasons for nonsatisfaction. In addition, subjective perceptions on education outcomes, for example as to whether a child is able to read, write, or compute, are also sometimes available. In some cases, additional interesting information may be available, for example on petty corruption in Cameroon (see appendix H for a discussion).

In the surveys for the 16 countries, with two surveys are available for Ghana, enough information is available on the type of provider relied upon for education in order to identify public, private secular and faith-inspired facilities, separately. This identification is at the core of the cross-country analysis presented in many of the chapters that follow, and it is also used for conducting more detailed work for Ghana and Burkina Faso. Details on the questions used to identify public providers, FISs, and private secular providers in the surveys/countries where the information is available are provided in appendix C.

As noted in appendix C, nongovernmental organizations (NGOs) have often been aggregated with faith-inspired providers for data reasons—that is, in a few countries the questionnaire simply lumps the two groups together, which in turn called for adding NGOs to FISs in the few cases where the two categories were separated in the questionnaires in order to maintain consistency. This does not affect the results substantially because the market share of NGOs is typically much smaller than that of faith-inspired providers, and it could also probably be argued that a nonnegligible share of the services provided by NGOs are actually faith inspired. Also, what is referred to as "secular providers" for simplicity consists of all providers that are neither faith inspired nor public. A change in terminology from "private secular" providers to "other private providers" was considered, but not adopted, for ease of presentation.

In all of the surveys identified with a "yes" in table 3.1, it is also feasible to assess which types of providers reach the poor. The poor will be defined in this study according to quintiles of well-being. In most cases, well-being is based on the level of consumption per capita or per equivalent adult of households, following the methodology officially adopted for poverty measurement and welfare analysis in each of the countries. In the cases where data on consumption are not available, following standard practice well-being is defined using an index of household wealth obtained from a factorial analysis of the assets owned by households and the characteristics of their dwelling. Although official poverty estimates vary between countries, in most countries the bottom two or three quintiles can be considered as representing the poor. For some topics, only a subset of countries have the necessary information in the survey data to conduct the analysis. For example, questions on the satisfaction of households with the education services that they receive will be analyzed for only seven of the countries in the sample, simply because that information is often lacking in most surveys.

Beyond providing a list of countries in table 3.1 where household survey information is available on FISs, it is worth describing a bit more the surveys that will be used for Ghana and Burkina Faso, given the more detailed work to be carried with these surveys. In Ghana, two main surveys are used for the analysis of the role of FISs in service delivery. The first survey is the Ghana Living Standards Survey (GLSS5) implemented in 2005/06. This is a multipurpose household survey covering demography, health, education, employment, migration, housing, agriculture activities, nonfarm self-employment, household expenditures, durable goods, and remittances and other incomes. The 2005/06 round of the survey was administrated to around 36,500 individuals belonging to 8,700 households. This nationwide sample is deemed representative at the level of the 10 regions.

The second survey is the large sample 2003 Core Welfare Indicator Questionnaire (CWIQ) survey (49,000 households). This survey provides information mainly on demography, health, education, employment, housing, and assets, but it does not include a consumption module, neither does it have information on the cost of education services. The two surveys complement each other nicely. For example, the GLSS5 is useful for analyzing, say, the cost of schooling, something that is not feasible with the CWIQ. By contrast, the CWIQ has information on the satisfaction of households with the services received, and the reasons for nonsatisfaction, something that is not available in the GLSS5. The fact that two surveys are available for Ghana is also useful for triangulating further some of the information that emerges from the surveys, for example in terms of market share and reach to the poor. Both surveys were implemented independently of each other using different sampling frame. If they tend to yield similar results, this is then reassuring.

In Burkina Faso, the main survey is the 2007 QUIBB, which stands for *Questionnaire des Indicateurs de Base du Bien-être*. This survey is very similar in design to the Ghana 2003 CWIQ, with essentially the same core modules on demography, health, education, employment, housing, and assets. The term QUIBB is actually a translation in French of the term "CWIQ," and both the QUIBB and CWIQ surveys are implemented by national Statistical Offices with technical support from the same division at the World Bank. As for the Ghana 2003 CWIQ, the Burkina Faso 2007 QUIBB does not have consumption data. The Burkina Faso CWIQ is not a very large sample survey like the Ghana 2003 CWIQ—but it has a sample size of 8,500 households, which is large enough.

Qualitative and Small Sample Data Collection

In addition to the analysis of household surveys and administrative data, this study also relies on qualitative and small sample data collected by the World Bank between April and June 2010 in both Ghana and Burkina Faso (see appendix D for details). These data were collected through interviews with parents, head teachers, and school principals for a total of eight or nine schools per country in one urban and one rural location in each of the two countries. The schools were selected with inputs from district education officials, but the main criteria was the requirement that there should be both public and faith-inspired schools in the areas where the qualitative work was conducted—this enabled individuals to discuss the advantages and disadvantages of different types of schools and explain the reasons why they chose specific schools facilities. Importantly, the selected areas had to have both Christian and Islamic schools, apart from public schools. The selection of the areas was done in such a way as to have at least two areas—one urban and one rural area—for each of the two countries.

Note that in the case of Ghana, faith-inspired schools—whether Christian or Islamic—can be categorized in two groups: public and private faith-inspired schools. Public faith-inspired schools are government owned and funded. They were originally established by FISs but later absorbed into the public education system. Since these schools are now government schools, they follow the national curriculum. Yet, at most of these schools additional religious instruction is provided beyond the core curriculum (for example, public Islamic schools teach religious topics and Arabic). By contrast, private faith-inspired schools were established by FISs and remain to-date for the most part without government support, as well as autonomous even if the curriculum at both the primary and secondary levels must follow accepted standards set by the Ghana Education Service.

The information from what is referred to in this study as the qualitative of fieldwork data comes from these in-depth interviews and focus groups carried in Ghana and Burkina Faso. A semi-structured questionnaire was used to interview individuals sending their children to the schools. Each interview took from one hour to one hour and a half, and focused in large part on the perceptions of the schools and the reasons that led individuals to choose one school versus another. Both responses to open-ended questions and closed questions will be used in the analysis. In the case of closed questions, quantitative statistics will be presented in percentage terms from those interviews, but it must be emphasized that the sample is small in both countries. A separate semi-structured questionnaire was also administered to the school principals and administrators as well as to a few teachers. A few additional interviews were conducted with key informants, such as officials from the Ministries of Education. More details on the fieldwork data and its sample size, as well as the questionnaires, are provided in appendix D.

Data Validity and Analysis

Validity of Household Survey Data on Service Delivery

A key contribution of this study consists in the systematic analysis of nationally representative household survey data to look at the role of FISs in education service provision. The advantage of household surveys is that their information can be used to not only obtain overall statistics, such as the market share of FISs in service delivery at the national level, but also statistics for various types of households, such as the market share of various providers for households belonging to different quintiles of well-being, from the poorest to the better off. Household surveys can also be used to look at marginal effects through econometric models—for example, it is feasible to look at the cost of attending a specific type of school controlling for individual and household characteristics that may also affect that cost.

But before discussing econometric issues, it is important to discuss the validity of household survey data for this study. As mentioned earlier, the findings obtained from household surveys are not always corresponding to the "conventional wisdom" on the role of FISs in service delivery in Sub-Saharan Africa. For example, estimates of the market share of FISs in education service delivery tend to be much lower using data from household surveys than is commonly assumed, at least in advocacy-focused networks. Does this mean that the estimates from household surveys are somehow biased, even if they are based on nationally representative surveys, or that alternatively the information obtained from other administrative data on facilities is flawed? An explanation for the much smaller market shares for FISs observed in household surveys could be that the identification of FISs by households in the surveys is flawed. It could be that households mistakenly identify facilities such as schools as belonging to the public sector, while the facilities are in fact faith inspired. This could happen for example if a school is publicly funded. There appears to be no clear evidence that this would indeed be the case, but if it were to be the case, it would be difficult to correct the existing data for potential issues of misidentification of FISs by households. What can be done though is to try to triangulate the results from a given survey with results from other surveys, and to look in more details at other sources of data, including administrative data, to see if the differences in results can be plausibly explained, as will be done in chapter 4.

Consider now another but related question. Assume for the sake of the argument that there may indeed be a bias, hopefully small, in the identification of FISs by households in household surveys, which would result in a lower market share for FISs in the surveys than is warranted. Is this likely to affect substantially other results, for example in terms of the analysis of whether FISs reach the poor or not, their cost in comparison to other facilities, the satisfaction of their users, or their performance? To a large extent, the position in this study is that this is not likely to be the case too much—these results will typically remain valid.

To understand why this is likely to be the case, consider the specific question of whether FISs tend to reach the poor proportionately more than public providers. Even if some FISs are misclassified by households as public schools in a household survey, to the extent that the likelihood of such misclassification is similar for all FISs, this should not affect substantially estimates of the extent to which various types of facilities reach the poor more than other types of facilities. This is because even if some FISs are misclassified by households as public facilities in a random way (the probability of misclassification is similar for all FISs), then the share of the beneficiaries that are poor in FISs is not affected.

As for public providers, if FISs serve the poor proportionately more (less) than public facilities, the erroneous inclusion of some FISs in their pool would lead to a higher (lower) share of beneficiaries of public facilities identified as poor than warranted, but the bias should be small because the number of FISs misclassified as public facilities would be small as a proportion of the total number of public facilities. This itself is because the market share of FISs is significantly smaller than that of public facilities, and because only a subset of FISs would be misclassified. In addition, if it turns out that the profile of beneficiaries according to their poverty status or level of well-being is similar between faith-inspired and public facilities, the bias generated by potential misclassification of the facilities by households would be even smaller. This is not to say that if there is a risk of bias, it should not be checked through triangulation, but rather that in most cases in this study, such potential bias related to misidentification of FISs in the surveys is not likely to affect results substantially.

As an example of triangulation to assess the validity of various sources of data for service delivery in education, consider data from the Ministry of Education of Ghana (Ministry of Education, Science and Sports 2009) for the academic year 2007/08. The data for education enrollment suggest that the CWIQ and GLSS5 surveys are not off the mark. In the 2007/08 academic year 83.0 percent of primary school students (593,819 out of 3,501,543) were enrolled in public schools in Ghana, and the proportion of public schools was at 76.9 percent (12,909 public primary schools versus 3,876 private schools). The proportion of students in public schools in 2007/08 estimated by the Ministry of Education is higher than it appears in both the CWIQ and the GLSS5 surveys, but not by too large a margin. In the 2003 CWIQ survey, 73.0 percent of students aged six to eleven go to government primary schools, and in the GLSS5, 76.9 percent go to public primary schools. The proportions of students going to faith-inspired schools in the two surveys are 5.0 percent and 6.7 percent, respectively. Given that many of the faith-inspired schools initially created in Ghana have long been publicly funded, and thus are now considered as public schools by the Ministry and probably by parents (it is not clear for most of these schools that they have retained their faith-inspired character), both the CWIQ and the GLSS5 survey appear to be capturing the market share of public, faith-inspired, and other private schools well, and thus are reliable, at least on average, to look at the characteristics of the various types of schools. Thus the order of magnitude of the market shares for public, private, and faith-inspired schools in the Ghana surveys seems reliable in terms of broad proportions.

Statistical and Econometric Analysis

This study aims to be accessible to a large public, including noneconomists, and especially practitioners interested in the area of religion and development. In some parts of the study however, regression analysis of survey data is provided. And throughout, basic statistics are computed from the household surveys. Because the analysis is based on household surveys, any estimation—whether through basic statistics or econometrics—entails standard errors. In the case of statistical tables, these standard errors are not reported in order to reduce the size of the tables. The reason why this can be done without much information loss is related to the nature of the variables being considered. Because most of the variables for which statistics are provided are categorical (they only take two values—zero and one), an approximation of the standard errors can be computed directly from the variable's mean values, which are provided in the tables, and the sample size of the surveys or group within the surveys being considered (see appendix E for details). In addition, in most cases, because the sample sizes are large, statistical estimates tend to have small standard errors. In the case of regressions, again to facilitate the lecture of the study, detailed results are provided in appendix G, while the text focuses on the parameters of interest.

Different types of regression analysis are used. For example, the model used for analyzing the probability of enrollment in various types of schools is a multinomial logit. The model for looking at the correlates of whether or not a child can read or write as a function of child, household, and other characteristics, including the type of school attended, is a probit. The models used for analyzing the cost of schooling is a tobit, given censoring at zero values. When analyzing variables that take a value between 0 percent and 100 percent, fractional logit estimation is relied upon. All of those models are relatively straightforward, and available in standard statistical packages. The Stata software was used for all estimations.

One important issue with regression analysis that must be briefly mentioned here is that of potential endogeneity bias due to self-selection into various types of service providers. If the dependent variable, such as the cost of a school, and one of the explanatory variables, such as the choice of school attended, are having an influence on each other, the regression models will produce estimates that are inconsistent and biased. For example, the cost that parents are ready to pay for their child's education depends on the features of the school chosen, but the choice of school itself also depends on its cost, and ignoring this will lead to a bias in the estimate of the impact of the type of school chosen on cost. In all such cases, in order to properly estimate the correlates of cost (or other dependent variables), it is necessary to first estimate the probability of attending different types of schools, and for this it is recommended to find another variable that is correlated with the explanatory variable (the type of school attended) conditioning on the other explanatory variables, but not with the dependent variable. This variable can then be used as an instrument in the estimation of the probability of attending different types of schools in order to produce consistent and unbiased estimates of the main regression, with bootstrapping in the second-stage regression.

In this study, in several regressions the leave-out mean/share of students attending different types of schools in the primary sampling unit in which a student or patient lives is used as an instrument for the choice of the school in the first stage regressions.[1] This is because the leave-out share is typically strongly correlated with the choice of a school (if only because it is an indication of the attractiveness of different types of schools in the vicinity of the household, and of the demand for these facilities), but it is unlikely to be correlated with learning outcomes beyond the fact that it affects the likelihood of going to a specific type of school. This idea of using the leave-out-mean for identification follows among others Ravallion and Wodon (2000).

Limited Scope of the Study

Focus on Service Delivery

When conceiving this study, a choice was made to focus on the relationship between faith and service delivery in education, as opposed to the broader question of the impact of faith on education outcomes. A key reason for not looking in details at the impact of faith on behaviors that affect human development was related to the limits of the survey data used for this study, and especially the lack of information beyond faith affiliation. The national household surveys used for this study provide information on human development outcomes, as well as on the type of service provider used, but not on people's faith apart from their broad faith affiliation. These surveys are therefore often not rich enough in terms of their questionnaire to assess in-depth what the impact of faith may be on various behaviors that affect education outcomes. When the only information available in the surveys is that of the faith affiliation of individuals or households, this leads to rather crude inferences about the impact of faith on behavior because the salience of a person's faith is not taken into account.

It is one thing to use statistical or regression analysis to assess whether faith-inspired schools have a better record than public and private secular facilities in terms of satisfaction among users, lower cost, or higher performance. It is also feasible to look at the impact of an individual's faith on where a parent sends children to school. But it would seem farfetched to try to look at the impact of faith, controlling for other household and individual characteristics, on outcomes such as, say, test scores. The likelihood that faith as observed in the survey through broad characteristics only would have a direct effect on test score controlling for other factors such the attainment level of the children, the education of the parents, or their income and wealth status, is probably low, and even if such an impact were somehow observed, its mechanisms of transmission would have to be studied further in order to understand what exactly is going on. The same holds to a large extent for simpler topics such as education attainment. If there is a reasonable presumption that faith may have a direct impact on outcomes, it may make sense to look at the impact of faith on such outcomes. But again, when surveys provide only information on the broad faith affiliation of an individual or household, what can be learned through regression analysis about the potential impact of faith on education outcomes is limited. Therefore, given the already broad scope of this study in matters of service delivery, it is best not to analyze here in details how faith affects directly or indirectly selected human development outcomes, but this could clearly be an area for further work.

Focus on Facilities-Based Services[2]

The term used so far in this study to identify faith-inspired providers of education services is FISs, which stands for faith-inspired schools, but could also stand for broader faith-inspired initiatives. This term is on purpose generic, and there is no intention in his study to discuss in any depth how various other terms could be used, or whether some terms are more appropriate than others for a specific purpose. Clearly, many terms have been used in the literature and will continue to be used. A review of religious health provision in Sub-Saharan Africa by Schmid et al. (2008) noted over 300 terms being used to describe various types of FISs engaged in healthcare in Africa. That list might grow further if the terminology used in education would be included.

Perhaps the alternative term that could have been used and that corresponds the most to what this study implies when referring to FISs is that of faith-based organizations (FBOs). As noted by Olivier (2011) in the case of health, six common meanings tend to be associated with FBO: (1) faith-forming entities whose primary function is the formation of faith or worship, (2) religious leaders, (3) religious nongovernmental organizations, (4) community-based religious initiatives, (5) networks, and (6) facilities. This itself is a quite heterogeneous list, and within that list, a religious nongovernmental organization is what is meant for the most part in this study when using the term FIS. This is because in much of the work that follows, the focus is on somewhat formal education facilities that provide services to households, rather than on other types of FISs. The term FIS was chosen over that of FBO or faith-based schools mainly because the use of "inspired" appears to be less restrictive than that of "based". But beyond those preferences which may well be idiosyncratic, in terms of the substantive findings of this study, they could have been associated as well with the use of the term FBO or faith-based schools.

Even if terminology is not essential in this study, it does not mean that it does not matter in general. In some cases terminology does matter, and advocates for one term versus another often feel strongly about this. Nevertheless, as far as research is concerned, the debate among academics over the term "FBO" (for example, Bradley 2009; Clarke 2006; Sider and Unruh 2004) may not have had much impact on policy (Olivier 2011). Today many terms tend to be used interchangeably, and this is not necessarily problematic. In this study, in large part because of the limits of the data available for analysis, the term FIS refers in most cases to a faith-inspired physical facility that provides education services, such as a school. The study also focuses implicitly essentially on day schools, as opposed to evening or other programs. This simplicity is why it is not necessary to enter into debates on terminology. But it also implies that there is clear limit to the scope of this study, in that it focuses for the most part on formal facilities, as opposed to many other types of informal institutions or initiatives that are faith inspired and that deal with education in one way or another.

Another issue of terminology that will not be debated in this study relates to what can be considered as faith inspired. The apparently simple binary distinction between religious and secular is itself problematic, as religiosity is often a matter of degree. For example, the World Council of Churches has differentiated between "faith-related organizations," "faith-background organizations," "faith-centeredorganizations" and "faith-saturated organizations" (Doupe 2005, see also Sider and Unruh 2004). In Africa especially, the division between the religious and the secular is far from obvious because religion remains embedded in everyday life, and is also integral to the character of many secular-classified organizations.

Some studies have attempted to assess FISs by ownership, for example by which denomination, faith tradition, or coordinating network the entity might belong to. This is also hazardous. In many countries faith-inspired schools are publicly funded, and in some cases ownership may not always be (or have been) clearly defined in the law, as is the case for the Democratic Republic of Congo. Classification is not value-free, and institutions and initiatives often adjust descriptions of their type and activities according to how they perceive it would be most useful to be understood in a particular situation or context. Classification has for example implications for access to resources, representation, and collaboration with governments. At one time it might be useful to be labeled an FIS or FBO to open certain funding doors, and at other times less so.

The point of this discussion is not that the distinctions such as the religious-secular classification should be ignored, but rather that one should be aware of the heterogeneity that prevails among FISs, and of the complexities of the realities on the ground. It should be clear that because of its focus on facilities-based services, this study should not be seen as descriptive of the entire engagement in education of FISs, as would be the case with a comprehensive account of the contribution of all FISs to various aspects of education provision. Such a comprehensive account falls beyond the scope of this study.

Conclusion

The objective of this chapter was to describe the data used in the study, as well as some of the methodological choices that have been made, both in terms of the techniques used, and in terms of the scope of the work. In terms of data, most of the work is based on an analysis of nationally representative multipurpose household surveys, with more in-depth work for Ghana and Burkina Faso. In addition to household survey data, the study also relies on administrative data from Ministries of Education and qualitative fieldwork information previously collected by the World Bank in April-June 2010 in both Ghana and Burkina Faso. In terms of methodology, it was suggested that the household survey data used for the analysis are valid for the purpose at hand, which is to discuss the role of FISs in service delivery. For example, the issue of misidentification of FISs by households is not likely to be too serious. A few other methodological issues related to standard errors and statistical significance, as well as to the risk of endogeneity bias in regression analysis were also mentioned.

While the data available seem appropriate for the purpose at hand, the data would have limits for discussing the broader topic of the impact of faith on a range of behaviors that affect education outcomes. This is because the information on faith available in the surveys is limited to the broad faith affiliations of individuals. The surveys used here have detailed information on education attainment and the services used by households for education—this is precisely the reason for using those surveys, but the surveys have limited information on faith. Surveys that focus on faith and values, such as the World Values Surveys or the surveys on religion conducted by the Pew Forum could be used for work on faith and selected behaviors and attitudes, but they are not useful to look at the role of FISs in service provision. It is because of the limits of the information available in the surveys used for this study that the focus is on service delivery, and not faith and education more broadly. Another limit of the study is that it focuses on facilities-based service delivery, and not on the wider range of faith-inspired initiatives in education that are not facilities based. The reason for this is again related to data—these initiatives, which are often local and community based, are typically not captured in household surveys. Nevertheless, despite these two main limits related to data, the scope of the study remains broad.

Notes

1. To be more price on what is meant by leave-out-mean, assume we want to compute the leave-out share (mean) of children attending school. We first define the way observations in a survey are to be grouped (alternatives include neighbourhoods, counties, and enumeration areas, among others), and then for every group and for each observation in the group, we compute the share of children attending a specific type of school in the group, excluding the observation being analyzed. The share computed as described is known as the leave-out mean. Note that each observation in the same group might have a different value for the leave-out mean. When computing the leave-out means or shares, the specific child or patient is excluded.
2. This section is based in part on work with Jill Olivier.

CHAPTER 4

Market Share

Introduction

Having explained the framework that guides this study and described the data and methodology used, the analysis of the role that faith-inspired schools (FISs) play in education in Sub-Saharan Africa starts with this chapter. Specifically, this chapter considers the question of the market share of FISs, while the next two chapters discuss questions regarding the reach to the poor of the various providers, as well as the cost for households to use the services provided.

In a loose way, one could say that chapters 4 through 6 are focused on the "supply side" of service delivery. By contrast chapter 7, on user satisfaction with the various types of providers, and the reasons for choosing specific providers (and especially faith-inspired providers) is mostly devoted to the "demand side" of service delivery. This is a loose characterization because for any of the questions considered we observe the result of some type of equilibrium between the supply of services and the demand for services. Nevertheless, it remains that the size of the public, private secular, and faith-inspired providers, as well as the cost of their services and who they reach are in large part the result of supply decisions by the management of various providers, while the satisfaction with the services received and the reasons for choosing specific providers relate more to the preferences of the households that demand these services, and are thus more related to the "demand side" of service delivery.

It is worth emphasizing at the outset that many private providers do not aim to increase their market share. Some private providers, and especially FISs, tend to be driven more by altruistic motives, as opposed to size or profit making. What matters to at least some of those providers is typically to serve the population with good quality services, and with a preferential option for the poor (this is a Christian term, but it is also often a core priority for Islamic facilities). Yet it is important to discuss market shares, if only to get a basic idea of the scope of the activities of various providers, especially given that some statements about market share appear to be off-track, especially in the case of FISs. Indeed, it is often stated that FISs account for about half of all education services provided in Sub-Saharan Africa. As mentioned in chapter 1, examples of statements to this effect include that of past World Bank President James Wolfensohn who suggested that "Half the work in education and health in Sub-Saharan Africa is done by the church" (quoted by Kitchen 2002). Similarly, a recent UNFPA (2009, see also UNFPA. 2004) report states that "there is clearly an important parallel faith-based universe of development, one which provides anywhere between 30–60% of healthcare and educational services in many developing countries." Many other examples of such statements could be given. There is some empirical basis for such statements, especially for healthcare, but it is often weak and the statements are problematic (see Olivier and Wodon 2012 in the case of market shares for healthcare).

The statements about the market share of FISs appear to be at odds with data collected from Ministries of Education by the UNESCO Institute of Statistics (UNESCO 2011). These data suggest that on average the market share of all private providers of primary education in African countries is in the 12 percent to 14 percent range for primary education, and at about 20 percent for secondary education. There is of course a lot of variance between countries in these market shares, but these are the average values across most countries in Sub-Saharan Africa for all private sector providers. Some 50 years ago faith-inspired providers did account for a large share of education services in many countries, but this share dropped with the expansion of public facilities. Jimenez and Lockheed (1995) suggest that in East Africa, the market share of all private schools dropped from 53 percent in 1965 to 20 percent in 1985, while the drop was from 26 percent in West Africa in 1965 to 18 percent in 1985.

The issue of the market share of FISs is actually not that essential—questions about the reach to the poor, cost, and performance of various providers are more important. The analysis presented in this chapter suggests that the market share of FISs, as well as secular private providers, is much smaller than is often believed, but this should not be considered in any way as stating that these providers do not play a fundamental role in the education systems of many African countries. They often do play a fundamental role, and this is precisely why it is better to clear the issue of the market share upfront. Indeed, suggesting that various private providers have a very high market share may actually undermine advocacy efforts for encouraging governments and donors to better support some private providers if it is clear that the advocacy or policy advice is based on data that suffers from serious flaws.

The rest of the chapter follows a structure replicated in subsequent chapters. Section 2 first provides cross-country evidence. Section 3 then provides additional evidence for Ghana and Burkina Faso. A brief conclusion follows.

Cross-Country Comparisons

Administrative Data on Market Share

Administrative data are available from the UNESCO Institute of Statistics (UIS) on the role of the private sector in education in Africa. A recent UIS publication provides estimates of the share of enrollment in private schools at both the primary and secondary levels circa 1999 and 2009 (UNESCO 2011). The data are reproduced in table 4.1. In the UIS report, private schools are defined as those schools that are controlled and managed by a private body such as a nongovernmental organization, a religious body, a special interest group, a foundation, or a business enterprise. Both nonprofit and for-profit schools are considered. Thus, what defines the public/private status of a school is who controls and manages the school, not who funds the school. Privately managed or controlled schools that are funded by the government are considered as private.

Table 4.1 Market Share Estimates from UIS Administrative Data, Education
percent

	Primary schools (ISCED1)		Secondary schools (ISCED 2–3)	
	1999	2009	1999	2009
Angola	n.a.	2.0^{-1}	n.a.	n.a.
Benin	7.2	9.1^{-1}	18.3	n.a.
Botswana	4.7	5.0^{-2}	4.1	3.0^{-1}
Burkina Faso	10.8	14.2	33.1	42.0
Burundi	1.3^{+2}	1.1	n.a.	8.8
Cameroon	27.7	22.8	31.6	22.2
Cape Verde	n.a.	0.4	n.a.	12.5
Central African Republic	35.5	13.8	n.a.	9.7
Chad	25.0	8.6	14.0	n.a.
Comoros	12.4	14.8^{-1}	46.2	n.a.
Congo, Rep.	10.0	35.4	8.7	n.a.
Cote d'Ivoire	11.6	10.7	36.2	n.a.
Congo, Dem. Rep.	n.a.	n.a.	n.a.	n.a.
Equatorial Guinea	32.8	47.1	23.2	n.a.
Eritrea	11.1	9.0	6.5	5.2
Ethiopia	n.a.	6.0	n.a.	8.7
Gabon	17.2	n.a.	29.3	n.a.
Gambia	13.7	19.5^{-1}	26.1	26.7^{-1}
Ghana	13.3	18.0	7.1	14.9
Guinea	14.7	26.3^{-1}	n.a.	23.3^{-1}
Guinea-Bissau	19.4	n.a.	12.8^{+1}	n.a.
Kenya	n.a.	10.6	n.a.	12.7
Lesotho	0.1	n.a.	n.a.	n.a.
Liberia	38.4	29.8^{-1}	37.2	57.6^{-1}
Madagascar	21.9	18.0	51.4^{+1}	40.3
Malawi	n.a.	n.a.	n.a.	n.a.
Mali	21.9	39.7	n.a.	32.3
Mauritius	23.8	27.2	73.5	55.8
Mozambique	n.a.	1.7	n.a.	11.5
Namibia	4.1	4.8	4.4	5.1
Niger	4.0	3.9	16.4	20.0

table continues next page

Table 4.1 Market Share Estimates from UIS Administrative Data, Education *(continued)*
percent

	Primary schools (ISCED1)		Secondary schools (ISCED 2–3)	
	1999	2009	1999	2009
Nigeria	6.5^{+1}	5.4^{-2}	28.9	13.7^{-2}
Rwanda	n.a.	2.5	42.5	31.9
Sao Tom & Pr.	n.a.	0.3	n.a.	1.8
Senegal	12.1	13.5	26.3^{+1}	19.8^{-1}
Seychelles	4.7	8.2	3.2	7.1
Sierra Leone	1.1^{+1}	n.a.	1.9^{+2}	6.9^{-2}
Somalia	n.a.	n.a.	n.a.	n.a.
South Africa	1.7	2.5^{-2}	2.3	n.a.
Swaziland	n.a.	n.a.	n.a.	n.a.
Togo	35.6	n.a.	17.7	n.a.
Uganda	n.a.	13.4	n.a.	51.5^{-1}
United Republic of Tanzania	0.2	1.5	n.a.	11.1
Zambia	n.a.	2.3	n.a.	2.6
Zimbabwe	88.1	n.a.	71.7	n.a.
Average (all countries, incl. Zimbabwe in 1999)	16.6	12.8	25.0	20.0

Source: UNESCO 2011.
Note: In the International Standard Classification of Education, ISCED-1 represents primary education, ISCED-2 lower secondary school, and ISCED-3 upper secondary schools. The upper scripts in the table indicate when the education system in a country differs from ISCED norms. n.a. = not applicable.

The share of students in private schools in table 4.1 is based on enrollment in those schools divided by total enrollment at the education level being considered. The reference period is the academic year ending in 2009 or the most recent year available between 2006 and 2009 (the same logic applies for the 1999 estimates). The data are obtained through the UIS Annual Education Survey sent by UNESCO to its member states. The UIS study notes that changes in reporting may occur between years, for example if community schools are classified as public schools in one year, and as private schools in another. Such changes may affect trends over time, but in most countries they should be minor. In 2009, out of the 45 countries listed, data on private market shares at the primary level are missing for 10 countries: the Democratic Republic of Congo, Gabon, Guinea-Bissau, Lesotho, Malawi, Sierra Leone, Somalia, Swaziland, Togo, and Zimbabwe (for four of these—the Democratic Republic of Congo, Malawi, Sierra Leone, and Swaziland, this study provides household survey-based estimates).

Of the remaining 35 countries in table 4.1, the market share of private schools is below 5 percent in 11 countries, and above 15 percent in 9 countries. The average market share for all countries with data in 2009 is 12.8 percent (simple average not weighted by country populations). For the countries with data in 1999, the average private market share is 16.6 percent, but this is driven up by Zimbabwe (without Zimbabwe, the average private market share is 14.3 percent).

At the secondary level, the average private market share in 2009 for the countries with data is at 20.0 percent, while it was at 25.0 percent for the year 1999, but this is again due in large part to data available for Zimbabwe in 1999, but not in 2009. As noted in the UNESCO report, when looking at the countries where data are available for both years, one observes a growing market share for private schools in most of the countries, especially at the secondary level. This can be interpreted as a sign of limited satisfaction on the part of parents with existing public schools, and it is likely that those who have been able to rely more on private schools come mostly from privileged backgrounds.

Household Survey Data for Education and Comparison with Administrative Data

Consider now estimates based on household surveys for primary and secondary education in table 4.2. The market shares for FISs range from 1.2 percent in Mali to 69.8 percent in the Democratic Republic of Congo for primary schools. The high market share in the Democratic Republic of Congo (and Sierra Leone) relates in part to the impact of conflict that led to state failure and an inability for public schools to function properly, but also to historical factors. Beyond these two countries, the highest market share for FISs is at 25.7 percent in Swaziland. The average market share for FISs is at 14.0 percent, versus 12.3 percent for secular private schools.

Table 4.2 Market Share Estimates from Multipurpose Surveys, Education
percent

	Public sector	Faith-inspired	Other private	Total private (1)	UIS estimate (2)	Difference with UIS (1)–(2)
			Primary education			
Burkina Faso, 2007	88.9	4.9	6.3	11.2	14.2	−3.1
Burundi, 2006	96.2	2.1	1.7	3.8	1.1	2.7
Cameroon, 2007	74.1	12.6	13.3	25.9	22.8	3.1
Congo, Dem. Rep., 2005	18.4	69.8	11.8	81.6	—	—
Ghana, 2003	73.8	4.7	21.5	26.2	18.0	8.2
Ghana, 2005/06	73.3	7.4	19.3	26.7	18.0	8.7
Kenya, 2005	90.2	2.3	7.5	9.8	10.6	−0.8
Malawi, 2004	81.0	17.2	1.9	19.0	—	—
Mali, 2006	85.0	1.2	13.8	15.0	39.7	−24.7
Niger, 2007	70.0	8.7	21.3	30.0	3.9	26.1
Nigeria 2003/04	77.2	2.5	20.3	22.8	5.4	17.4
Congo, Rep., 2005	73.3	3.1	23.6	26.7	35.4	−8.7
Senegal, 2005	86.1	7.0	7.0	13.9	8.2	5.7
Sierra Leone, 2003/04	37.3	54.9	7.7	62.7	—	—
Swaziland, 2009/10	65.5	25.7	8.9	34.6	—	—
Uganda, 2010	75.0	2.4	22.7	25.0	13.4	11.6
Zambia, 2004	88.7	2.8	8.4	11.3	2.3	9.0
Average (using Ghana average)	73.8	14.0	12.3	26.2	14.6	3.9

table continues next page

Table 4.2 Market Share Estimates from Multipurpose Surveys, Education *(continued)*
percent

	Public sector	Faith-inspired	Other private	Total private (1)	UIS estimate (2)	Difference with UIS (1)–(2)
				Secondary education		
Burkina Faso, 2007	66.9	8.7	24.4	33.1	42.0	−8.9
Burundi, 2006	83.7	3.2	13.1	16.3	8.8	7.5
Cameroon, 2007	73.5	5.7	20.8	26.5	22.2	4.3
Congo, Dem. Rep., 2005	21.5	66.0	12.5	78.5	—	—
Ghana, 2003	84.7	3.2	12.1	15.3	14.9	0.4
Ghana, 2005/06	78.1	6.5	15.4	21.9	14.9	7.0
Kenya, 2005	81.0	6.2	12.8	19.0	12.7	6.3
Malawi, 2004	70.2	6.4	23.4	29.9	—	—
Mali, 2006	89.4	0.2	10.3	10.6	32.3	−21.7
Niger, 2007	81.8	0.8	17.4	18.2	20.0	−1.8
Nigeria 2003/04	84.0	1.2	14.7	16.0	13.7	2.3
Congo, Rep., 2005	77.4	1.1	21.5	22.6	8.7	13.9
Senegal, 2005	82.0	5.7	12.3	18.1	19.8	−1.8
Sierra Leone, 2003/04	54.9	41.6	3.6	45.2	—	—
Swaziland, 2009/10	74.0	19.6	6.4	26.0	—	—
Uganda, 2010	47.5	3.5	49.0	52.5	51.5	0.9
Zambia, 2004	92.5	3.8	3.7	7.5	2.6	4.9
Average (using Ghana average)	72.6	11.2	16.2	27.4	20.8	0.8

Source: Estimates based on national surveys. See Tsimpo and Wodon 2013b.

How do the UIS statistics compare with the estimates from household surveys used in this study? For the countries where estimates are available from both the surveys and the UIS data, the average difference in the estimates of private market share is 3.9 percent, which is not bad. The average private market share observed in the surveys is higher than the average share reported to the UIS by Ministries of Education, and this is what one would expect. Indeed, it is likely that some schools that do provide services to households are not recorded by Ministries of Education, because they operate without any official recognition. In some of the countries, the correspondence between the surveys and the UIS data is good, and this is the case for the two focus countries in this study. In Burkina Faso, the difference in market share is 3.1 percent, and in Ghana, it is at 8.2 percent and 8.7 percent depending on the survey (as compared to the estimate for 2009 in the UIS data), which still seems acceptable. In a few countries, the differences are very large, especially for Mali and Niger. In such cases, it is likely that the differences are due to a lack of comparability in the classifications used for the surveys and the administrative data.

What about secondary education? Mali is again the country with the smallest market share, and the highest market share is obtained for the Democratic Republic of Congo. The average market share for FISs is at 11.2 percent, versus 16.2 percent for private secular schools. For the countries where estimates are available from both the surveys and the UIS data, the average difference in the estimates of private market share is only 0.8 percent, but this hides large differences for some countries. The average private market share observed in the surveys is again higher than the average share reported to the UIS by Ministries of Education. In Burkina Faso, the difference in market share is higher than before, at 8.9 percent, but more importantly the level of the market share of private schools is much higher at the secondary level than at the primary level. In Ghana, especially with the Core Welfare Indicators Questionnaire (CWIQ) survey, the difference in market share between the surveys and the UIS data is smaller than at the primary level. Overall, for the purpose of this study, it seems that the survey data provide a sound basis for analysis.

Additional Evidence for Ghana and Burkina Faso

In Ghana, no administrative estimates appear to be available on the number of students served by various types of FISs.[1] However, in the case of Islamic schools, a report by USAID (2007) suggests that 1,418 Islamic schools under the supervision of Islamic Education Unit (IEU) at the Ghana Education Service (GES) were serving 213,893 children at the time of the study (for a brief discussion of the various types of Islamic schools in Ghana, see chapter 3). Of those schools, 497 are kindergartens, 699 are primary schools, and 255 are junior secondary schools. If one assumes no differences in size between the schools at the various levels of education, this would yield a total of about 105,000 primary school students in IEU Islamic schools, or about 2.5 percent of total primary school enrollment. Unfortunately, data in the Ghana Living Standard Survey, Fifth Round (GLSS5) are available only on the share of students attending private religious schools, and not by faith affiliation. Still, given that Christian schools have traditionally had a larger footprint than Islamic schools in Ghana, the market share for FISs in primary education estimated at 4.5 percent in the 2003 Core Welfare Indicators Questionnaire (CWIQ) is probably too low. The market share for FISs of 7.2 percent in the GLSS5 is likely to be closer to the true market share. Islamic leaders interviewed for the USAID report also suggest that there may be another 3,000 non-IEU Islamic schools, but these schools mostly attract students for evening or week end classes, while the students attend public schools during the day (on Islamic education in Ghana, see also Iddrisu, 2002, 2005).

In the case of Burkina Faso, detailed administrative information from the Ministry of Education is available as to the market of faith-inspired schools. The figures in table 4.3 suggest that for the school year 2008/09, private primary schools account for 14.2 percent of all students, 17.9 percent of schools and 19.6 percent of teachers. The information is also available separately for private secular, private Catholic, private Islamic, and private Protestant schools. The corresponding estimates obtained from the 2007 QUIBB survey, which distinguishes between the various types of faith-inspired schools, are also provided in table 4.3. The market share of private secular schools is slightly higher in the survey than in administrative records (6.3 percent nationally versus 5.2 percent), but it is lower for Islamic schools (2.6 percent in the survey versus 5.5 percent according

Table 4.3 Market Share by Type of Primary School, Burkina Faso
percent

Type of school	Administrative data 2008/09			Household survey 2007 (students only)		
	Students	Institutions	Teachers	Urban	Rural	National
Public	85.8	82.1	80.4	69.7	94.9	88.9
Private Secular	5.2	4.2	5.8	22.1	1.3	6.3
Private Catholic	1.6	1.3	1.6	5.2	0.5	1.6
Private Islamic	5.5	10.8	10.4	1.1	3.1	2.6
Private Protestant	1.8	1.5	1.7	2.0	0.3	0.7
All Faith-inspired	8.9	13.6	13.7	8.3	3.9	4.9
All Private	14.2	17.9	19.6	30.3	5.1	11.1
All Schools	100.0	100.0	100.0	100.0	100.0	100.0

Source: MENA, Office of Research and Planning and QUIBB 2007. See Gemignani and Wodon 2013.

Table 4.4 Trends in Primary School Enrolment by Type of School, Burkina Faso

	1997–2008	2006/07	2008/09
All Primary	776,691	1,561,258	2,047,630
Private			
Secular	37,875 (4.9%)	84,347 (5.4%)	107,222 (5.2%)
Islamic	24,823 (3.2%)	82,396 (5.3%)	113,580 (5.5%)
Protestant	13,342 (1.7%)	21,830 (1.4%)	37,053 (1.8%)
Catholic	3,110 (0.4%)	23,457 (1.5%)	32,207 (1.6%)

Source: Ministry of Education of Burkina Faso.

to the Ministry of Education) as well as for Protestant schools (0.7 percent in the survey versus 1.8 percent according to the Ministry). For Catholic schools, the same share is observed in the survey and in the administrative data (1.6 percent). It is also worth noting that in Burkina Faso as is the case in Ghana, the survey data suggest that the market share of FISs is substantially higher in urban than in rural areas. The administrative data suggest that Islamic schools tend to be much smaller than other schools (compare the share of students versus the share of schools), which may also explain why they tend to have more teachers per student than other types of schools (on Islamic education in Burkina Faso, see also Ouedraogo, 2008).

Data are also available in Burkina Faso about the growth of the various types of schools (table 4.4). Since the late 1990s, both Catholic schools, with their perceived academic strengths, and Islamic schools, with their popular appeal, have grown in market share. Protestant schools have about the same market share in 2008/09 as compared to 1997/98, and private secular schools also gained slightly. Note that a policy of free and compulsory basic education was adopted in 2007 for publicly funded schools, but this does not seem to have affected fundamentally the various market shares between 2007/08 and 2008/09. As already mentioned, overall the different types of private schools in

2008/09 had a combined market share of 14.2 percent in 2008/09, versus 10.2 percent in 1996–2007.

Conclusion

The purpose of this chapter was to assess the market share of FISs as compared to other education providers in Africa, with additional work for Ghana and Burkina Faso. It is often suggested that FISs provide close to half of all education services in the region. The evidence to this effect is very weak. Household survey data suggest a market share of FISs for primary education of about 14.0 percent on average in the countries where information has been collected for this study, and this is reduced to 11.2 percent for secondary education, with large differences between countries. When factoring in the role of private secular providers, the household survey data are broadly consistent with the estimates obtained for the market share of the private sector as a whole, as measured in administrative data collected by Ministries of Education for the UNESCO Institute of Statistics.

Note

1. Administrative data actually appear to be available at least in principle on enrolment in faith-inspired schools in the Education Management Information Systems, but it is not clear whether the data has been coded and it was not feasible to obtain this information from the Ministry of Education.

CHAPTER 5

Reach to the Poor and Vulnerable

Introduction

While it is common to state that faith-inspired schools (FISs) provide a large share of education services in Sub-Saharan Africa, it is also often suggested that they provide services in priority for the poor and vulnerable, especially in rural areas. Again, the empirical evidence to back such statements is rather thin, mostly anecdotal, and often outdated.

The issue of whether FISs reach the poor and vulnerable is probably more important than that of their market share. For a Ministry, being able to reach the poor and vulnerable, especially in remote areas, is important to ensure universal service, including within the context of the Millennium Development Goals (MDGs). If in some areas FISs may be able to contribute to this goal, and possibly more so than existing public facilities, this would be a major comparative advantage for FISs which would appear to warrant support, instead of duplication of efforts by locating new public facilities in those areas if they are already served. Even more importantly, for the FISs themselves, the ability to reach the poor and vulnerable is fundamental, given that some form of preferential option for the poor is a core component of their *ethos*. But what does it mean exactly to reach the poor? How can household survey data help in assessing whether FISs indeed reach the poor? At least four different interpretations of reaching the poor and vulnerable can be considered.

A first question is whether in their own clientele, FISs serve the poor—as traditionally defined on the basis of the consumption per equivalent adult of households, or when that is not available, on the basis of an index of household wealth—more than other population groups. This is a traditional benefit incidence analysis question, which can be answered by estimating whether the share of the services of FISs that are used by individuals from poor households is smaller or larger than the share of the services used by individuals from wealthier households. In the case of postprimary education, it is doubtful that FISs will reach the poor in this specific way, simply because the cost of education tends to be high for the poor, resulting in lower demand for those services among the poor than among the better-off. Thus, most postprimary education facilities, whether public, faith inspired, or private secular, will typically not reach the poor more than other groups in absolute terms due to the cost of their services which may not be affordable for the (very) poor. The case of primary education is a bit different, especially now that it is often free, at least in terms of direct fees (not in terms of other expenditures or opportunity costs) in public schools. In the case of primary education, if better off households send their children to private secular schools, and if a country has reached relatively high levels of primary school enrolment, then public schools will often reach the poor more than the better off in absolute terms. Where FISs fall depends on their characteristics and those of the country in which they operate—in some cases faith-inspired primary schools may reach the poor more than other groups in absolute terms, while in others they may not (this will depend in large part on their cost for households). In addition, the reach to the poor of faith-inspired schools is typically lower at the secondary than at the primary level, as is the case for other education providers.

A second question is whether FISs serve the poor proportionally more than other providers—namely public and private secular facilities. This is equivalent to asking a relative benefit incidence analysis question. Even if FISs do not reach the poor more than other groups in absolute terms, they may reach the poor more than other providers. This would mean that the share of the poor among the users of FISs would be larger than that of other types of providers. Clearly, because many secular private providers cater to the better off, one could expect that FISs would reach the poor more than other private providers. But whether they reach the poor proportionately more than public providers is an open question. Indeed, even if FISs would like to focus on the poor, this may not be feasible if they do not benefit from financial support from governments or various types of donors. Providing services of good quality is not cheap, and in the absence of external support, few FISs would be able to remain financially sustainable without cost recovery mechanisms. A lower level of financial support for FISs may require a higher level of cost recovery from the users of services, which may drive the poor away from faith-inspired facilities when the cost becomes too high. But FISs may also benefit from more funding if they are increasingly integrated within national education systems, although they may have less freedom in some areas. For example they may not be able to cross-subsidize the poor by charging more to the better off, and this may affect negatively their ability to serve the poor. While it is difficult to analyze the many factors that may lead FISs to be able (or not) to serve the poor proportionately more than other providers, simply measuring whether they do so (or not) is straightforward with household surveys.

A third and more difficult question is whether FISs make special efforts to reach the poor. This is the question that is probably closest in spirit to the concept of the preferential option for the poor in Catholic social thought. While the first two questions will be dealt with exclusively in this chapter, the third question will be dealt both in this chapter and in chapter 6 devoted to the cost of the services provided by FISs, simply because cost—together with quality—is a key determinant of whether the poor are able to benefit from the services of FISs.[1] That is, some evidence on special efforts by FISs to reach the poor will be discussed in this chapter, but this complex question will also be dealt with in chapter 6.

Finally, a fourth question is whether FISs succeed in serving others in need who may not be defined as poor in the traditional sense, but are vulnerable. This is a complex question, not only because all of the three distinctions made earlier could apply here as well, but also because who is vulnerable depends on the type of vulnerability considered. One example would be to assess whether FISs serve orphans. Entire studies could be (and have been) devoted to these questions (see Olivier and Wodon 2012 for a review on some of the work on human immunodeficiency virus-acquired immune deficiency syndrome [HIV-AIDS]). Given the limited scope of this study, it is not feasible to consider various types of vulnerabilities and assess to which extent FISs are able to help individuals and households in these areas. All that can be done is to give some examples. This is done here by discussing the results from a quantitative analysis of the types of schools that welcome children with disabilities in Ghana.

As in chapter 4 and the next two chapters, in order to tackle these four different but related questions, the chapter provides first cross-country evidence as to whether FISs reach the poor more than other facilities in absolute terms, or in comparison to public and private secular facilities. Thereafter the focus is on additional evidence for Ghana and Burkina Faso. A conclusion follows.

Cross-Country Evidence

As in the previous chapter devoted to estimates of market share, this section uses data from nationally representative household surveys whose questionnaire modules for education are detailed enough to permit the identification of FISs among the various types of service providers that households rely upon. The focus is on the first two questions mentioned in the introduction—do FISs reach the poor more, in absolute or relative terms, with the poor defined in the traditional way through their level of consumption (or through an index of asset-based wealth when consumption is not available). That is, is the absolute share of the poor in the clientele of FISs higher than the share of other household groups? Second, are the services provided by FISs used by the poor proportionately more than the services made available by other providers?

In table 5.1, data are provided on the share of the users of the services provided by FISs by quintiles of well-being (the sum of the five estimates in each row is equal to 100 percent).[2] Although poverty estimates vary between countries, in most countries the bottom two or three quintiles can be considered as representing the poor. The evidence from the 16 countries suggests that for the most part, FISs do not serve the poor more than wealthier groups in absolute terms, and they may also not reach the poor proportionately more than public facilities.

Table 5.1 Benefit Incidence for Education by Type of Provider
percent

	Primary education					Secondary education				
	Q1	Q2	Q3	Q4	Q5	Q1	Q2	Q3	Q4	Q5
	Burkina Faso, 2007									
Public	12.6	17.9	21.6	23.5	24.4	4.4	5.6	14.8	23.1	52.0
Faith-inspired	8.1	6.3	17.0	23.8	44.8	1.1	2.5	8.8	19.5	68.1
Private secular	2.3	2.9	7.1	15.8	71.9	0.3	1.9	4.9	15.7	77.2
Total	11.8	16.4	20.5	23.0	28.4	3.1	4.4	11.9	21.0	59.6
	Burundi, 2006									
Public	22.7	22.7	21.2	20.1	13.3	22.7	22.7	21.2	20.1	13.3
Faith-inspired	27.9	21.7	16.6	19.6	14.2	27.9	21.7	16.6	19.6	14.2
Private secular	10.0	11.6	15.5	9.2	53.7	10.0	11.6	15.5	9.2	53.7
Total	22.6	22.5	21.0	19.9	14.0	22.6	22.5	21.0	19.9	14.0
	Cameroon, 2007									
Public	27.4	25.4	21.9	16.5	8.8	10.0	18.0	23.0	25.0	24.0
Faith-inspired	11.9	22.0	25.3	22.8	18.1	1.1	8.4	22.6	27.5	40.4
Private secular	2.5	8.6	17.3	27.8	43.8	1.9	7.1	16.7	30.1	44.2
Total	22.2	22.7	21.7	18.8	14.6	7.8	15.2	21.7	26.2	29.1
	Democratic Republic of Congo, 2005									
Public	23.4	21.0	19.9	20.9	14.9	18.4	18.5	20.8	20.9	21.5
Faith-inspired	23.5	22.6	20.9	18.5	14.6	20.7	19.5	20.7	19.1	20.1
Private secular	14.3	15.8	16.7	23.3	29.9	8.5	11.9	20.4	24.4	34.8
Total	22.4	21.5	20.2	19.5	16.4	18.7	18.3	20.7	20.1	22.2
	Ghana, 2003									
Public	23.1	26.6	22.4	17.4	10.5	9.6	19.0	25.9	26.2	19.3
Faith-inspired	17.1	24.8	23.1	19.6	15.5	11.4	15.0	28.6	26.0	19.1
Private secular	5.3	15.6	24.2	30.2	24.7	4.0	14.8	22.9	32.9	25.4
Total	19.0	24.1	22.8	20.2	13.8	8.9	18.4	25.7	27.0	20.0
	Ghana, 2005/06									
Public	25.6	25.2	22.7	16.9	9.7	14.9	20.3	23.8	22.7	18.4
Faith-inspired	7.4	14.1	18.4	30.4	29.8	4.3	11.9	19.1	30.5	34.2
Private secular	8.0	13.9	21.4	28.3	28.4	6.3	15.4	16.8	28.7	32.8
Total	20.8	22.2	22.2	20.1	14.8	12.9	19.0	22.4	24.1	21.7
	Senegal, 2005									
Public	22.0	20.3	20.2	19.0	18.5	13.3	12.9	17.1	23.4	33.4
Faith-inspired	13.0	11.1	11.9	16.4	47.5	6.8	9.2	8.9	18.0	57.2
Private secular	2.0	5.6	7.9	24.3	60.3	3.8	7.7	7.6	21.4	59.5
Total	20.0	18.7	18.8	19.2	23.4	11.8	12.0	15.5	22.8	37.9
	Sierra Leone, 2003/04									
Public	17.1	16.1	24.2	22.7	19.9	4.6	8.0	14.4	22.9	50.2
Faith-inspired	24.4	21.8	22.0	19.7	12.2	9.1	17.0	20.8	24.2	28.9
Private secular	21.1	20.9	9.2	19.5	29.4	1.8	8.0	6.6	8.9	74.7
Total	21.4	19.6	21.8	20.8	16.4	6.4	11.8	16.8	22.9	42.2

table continues next page

Table 5.1 Benefit Incidence for Education by Type of Provider *(continued)*
percent

	Primary education					Secondary education				
	Q1	Q2	Q3	Q4	Q5	Q1	Q2	Q3	Q4	Q5
	Swaziland, 2009/10									
Public	25.3	23.0	23.6	17.2	10.8	16.7	22.1	21.9	23.7	15.6
Faith-inspired	26.9	23.5	20.0	18.6	11.1	16.5	14.6	18.1	28.7	22.2
Private secular	8.3	12.6	15.1	23.9	40.1	7.7	1.8	16.8	9.9	63.8
Total	24.2	22.2	21.9	18.2	13.4	16.1	19.3	20.8	23.8	20.0
	Kenya, 2005									
Public	24.0	23.9	21.7	18.2	12.2	8.7	16.1	21.7	26.7	26.9
Faith-inspired	11.6	17.8	12.5	23.4	34.7	5.7	12.1	23.0	28.6	30.7
Private secular	6.7	10.9	12.3	24.7	45.5	6.5	13.6	23.5	14.7	41.7
Total	22.4	22.8	20.8	18.8	15.2	8.2	15.5	22.0	25.3	29.1
	Zambia, 2004									
Public	19.8	21.1	20.7	20.8	17.6	12.5	16.5	18.8	23.8	28.4
Faith-inspired	11.6	16.9	21.5	27.7	22.3	11.7	7.5	14.1	17.3	49.4
Private secular	12.3	12.6	12.4	18.4	44.4	1.2	3.4	12.3	17.4	65.8
Total	18.9	20.2	20.0	20.8	20.0	12.1	15.7	18.4	23.3	30.6
	Malawi, 2004									
Public	23.4	23.0	21.5	18.4	13.8	9.2	13.9	16.4	25.7	34.8
Faith-inspired	23.3	21.2	19.6	21.2	14.6	6.4	1.0	8.6	21.2	62.8
Private secular	3.3	4.7	10.5	14.2	67.3	3.8	9.5	10.2	18.7	57.8
Total	23.0	22.3	21.0	18.8	15.0	7.7	12.1	14.5	23.8	42.0
	Congo, Rep., 2005									
Public	27.2	26.6	21.3	17.3	7.6	20.5	22.7	21.7	20.6	14.5
Faith-inspired	13.7	13.3	30.1	25.7	17.3	20.8	28.0	13.6	30.0	7.6
Private secular	9.9	16.7	22.4	23.4	27.6	5.3	13.3	20.3	31.0	30.1
Total	22.7	23.9	21.8	19.0	12.6	17.2	20.8	21.3	22.9	17.8
	Nigeria 2003/04									
Public	16.7	17.8	22.5	23.3	19.8	12.4	15.5	19.0	24.0	29.1
Faith-inspired	16.9	20.9	18.4	22.6	21.2	25.8	8.3	9.0	15.4	41.5
Private secular	9.8	13.3	14.4	23.1	39.4	6.7	9.5	14.1	24.6	45.1
Total	15.3	16.9	20.8	23.2	23.8	11.7	14.5	18.2	24.0	31.6
	Niger, 2007									
Public	18.8	20.0	20.7	21.7	18.7	11.9	12.2	13.9	23.2	38.8
Faith-inspired	17.2	15.1	19.3	18.4	30.0	0.0	0.0	23.7	26.3	50.0
Private secular	13.5	16.8	18.2	23.7	27.8	1.5	2.8	3.0	4.8	87.9
Total	17.6	18.9	20.1	21.9	21.6	10.0	10.4	12.1	20.0	47.4
	Mali, 2006									
Public	15.4	19.5	20.4	24.1	20.6	6.6	10.5	13.7	28.3	41.0
Faith-inspired	1.2	4.8	19.8	16.7	57.5	0.0	0.0	69.7	30.3	0.0
Private secular	5.0	7.4	6.3	21.6	59.8	2.0	5.2	6.6	21.5	64.8
Total	13.8	17.6	18.4	23.7	26.5	6.1	9.9	13.1	27.6	43.3

table continues next page

Table 5.1 Benefit Incidence for Education by Type of Provider *(continued)*
percent

	Primary education					Secondary education				
	Q1	Q2	Q3	Q4	Q5	Q1	Q2	Q3	Q4	Q5
	Uganda, 2010									
Public	26.9	23.9	21.5	18.4	9.3	13.0	16.3	20.5	24.5	25.8
Faith-inspired	12.6	25.0	16.8	23.5	22.0	5.1	10.6	29.5	16.2	38.7
Private secular	8.9	14.4	19.0	23.0	34.7	6.3	9.1	13.3	22.8	48.5
Total	22.5	21.8	20.8	19.5	15.4	9.5	12.5	17.3	23.4	37.3
	Average									
Public	21.7	21.8	21.6	19.9	15.0	12.3	15.7	19.0	23.8	29.2
Faith-inspired	16.0	17.7	19.5	21.5	25.3	10.4	10.9	20.7	23.1	34.9
Private secular	8.5	11.8	14.2	21.6	43.9	4.5	8.2	13.2	19.1	54.9
Total	20.0	20.7	20.8	20.3	18.2	11.2	14.6	18.1	23.3	32.8

Source: Estimates based on national household surveys. See Tsimpo and Wodon 2013b.
Note: For the overall average, the data for Ghana are the average for the two surveys (Core Welfare Indicators Questionnaire [CWIQ] and Ghana Living Standard Survey, Fifth Round [GLSS5]).

On average, for primary education, 16.0 percent of the clientele of FISs belongs to the bottom quintile, versus 25.3 percent in the top quintile. In computing these averages across the countries in the sample, the two survey data points for Ghana are themselves averaged. Note that some of the country estimates by quintile may have large standard errors, especially when the market share of FISs is smaller. But even if one takes out from the regional average the countries where the market share is very low, the results remain qualitatively the same. For secondary education, as expected (given that the poor tend to have lower educational attainment) the differences are even larger between quintiles, with 10.4 percent of students in faith-inspired schools belonging to the bottom quintile, versus 34.9 percent in the top quintile. Also, while in some countries faith-inspired schools are located more in urban areas, the reverse is observed in other countries.

What is likely to be at the source of those findings is the fact that the poor are less able than wealthier households to afford the cost of schooling (direct fees, indirect costs for uniforms and transport for example, and opportunity costs). While this is especially the case at higher levels of schooling, it also plays out at the primary level. Also, some FISs tend to cater to the well-to-do with an education of higher quality, but at a higher cost. There are again differences between countries, as expected. In Cameroon, the very poor tend not to rely on FISs much, and this is also the case in Burkina Faso, Mali, Senegal, Kenya, the Republic of Congo, Uganda, and Zambia. By contrast, in Burundi, Swaziland, and Malawi, participation by the very poor in FISs is much higher, at least at the primary level. Note that in the case of Ghana, the two surveys provide quite different estimates of the benefit incidence of FISs. The benefit incidence estimates for FISs are much more favourable to the poor when using the Core Welfare Indicators Questionnaire (CWIQ) survey than is the case when relying on data from the

Ghana Living Standard Survey, Fifth Round (GLSS5). This issue will be discussed in more details in section 3.

How do FISs compare to public facilities on average across the 16 countries? The benefit incidence by quintile for FISs is less propoor that for public facilities, for both primary and secondary schools. For example, as mentioned earlier, on average 16.0 percent of the primary education services provided by FISs reach children in the bottom quintile, and the proportion that reaches the second quintile is 17.7 percent. For public facilities, the corresponding shares are 21.7 percent and 23.8 percent. At the secondary level, only 10.4 percent of the services provided by FISs reach children in the bottom quintile, and the proportion is virtually the same in the second quintile (10.9 percent). For public schools, the corresponding shares are 12.3 percent and 15.7 percent. On the other hand, as expected, the services provided by faith-inspired schools are less titled towards better off children than is the case for private secular schools, for which 43.9 percent of the students in primary schools and 54.9 percent of the students in secondary schools come from households belonging to the top quintile.

To give a better appreciation for the high degree of heterogeneity between countries as to whether FISs reach the poor, consider the case of two very different countries: the Democratic Republic of Congo and Cameroon. The Democratic Republic of Congo is a case of an education system where most children live in poverty and where FISs have a large market share due in part to state failure. As noted by Backiny-Yetna and Wodon (2009b), the aftermath of independence was marked by political instability in the Democratic Republic of Congo, but the country was relatively peaceful and growing. From the mid-1960s to the mid-1970s, school enrollment grew, fueled not only by population growth but also by gains in enrollment rates, at an annual rate of five percent in primary, 19 percent in secondary, and 24 percent in tertiary education (World Bank 2005). Enrollment growth was reduced between the mid-1970s and mid-1990s due in part to an economic crisis triggered by a decline in copper prices. Thereafter, the civil war that followed the end of the 32-year Mobutu regime had a devastating effect on the economy, the population (3.0–5.5 million deaths were related directly or indirectly to the war), and human development.

Primary and secondary education in the Democratic Republic of Congo are provided by government schools (*écoles non-conventionées*), faith-inspired schools (*écolesconventionnées*), and private schools. Government and faith-inspired schools receive subsidies and are considered public schools. Private schools do not benefit from state support. The term "publicly supported," although technically correct, is however somewhat of a misnomer in the Democratic Republic of Congo, because most of the costs of education are borne by households. Indeed public financing for education has declined substantially and funding for education is very limited. As noted in World Bank (2005), the relationship between the government and religious institutions has however not been clearly defined. Private schools, including faith-inspired schools, were nationalized in 1974, but only for three years after which the government entered into an agreement with the four major religious networks (Roman Catholic, Protestant, Kimbanguiste, and Islamic). The agreement stipulates that faith-inspired schools must follow the public curriculum and norms on class size, teacher qualifications and salaries, and student assessment. In principle, the schools belong to the state even if they are managed by religious organizations. A 1986 law that gave broad authority to the Ministry of Education does not mention the religious school networks, even though a National Council of Education with representation from both the government and the religious networks was later created to coordinate national policy.

In practice, each religious network has its own structure and manages its schools. Each network also has to rely for the most part on its own resources to pay for the schools and teachers, with parents providing the bulk of the funding through various levies. The limited resources available to pay teachers, renovate the schools, reduce overcrowding, and provide instructional materials are a key factor leading to poor quality in education. Using data on perceptions of literacy and numeracy, Backiny-Yetna and Wodon (2009b) suggest low performance and few differences in performance between FISs and government schools. The analysis also suggests few differences by level of well-being in the students enrolled in FISs and government schools. One could thus say that FISs do not reach the poor more than government schools, but that would miss the point. In the case of the Democratic Republic of Congo, FISs serve the poor more in absolute terms than better-off households, simply because the overwhelming majority of the population is poor. And in addition, with about 70 percent of the students in faith-inspired schools, the school system is essentially faith inspired, and remained functioning in large part because FISs continued their work during the civil war.

At another extreme, consider the case of Cameroon, a lower-middle-income country, where fewer children live in poverty (even if poverty remains high, as discussed by Backiny-Yetna et al. 2009a). In Cameroon, about one in ten students attends a faith-inspired school. As was the case in the Democratic Republic of Congo, the state provides subsidies to both government and faith-inspired schools, but not to private schools. However, the subsidies per student provided by the state to faith-inspired schools are typically lower than the subsidies provided to public schools. This means that FISs have to raise more funds than public schools to be financially sustainable, which makes them more expensive for parents than public schools and results in a weaker targeting performance in reaching the poor.

Backiny-Yetna and Wodon (2009a) use the 2007 survey for Cameroon to analyze who FISs serve, how much parents have to pay for their children to attend FISs, and what the performance of FISs is, in comparison to public and secular private schools.[3] The focus of the analysis is on cost. While the data suggest that secular private schools are by far the most expensive, they also suggest that faith-inspired schools are significantly more expensive than public schools in both urban and rural areas. Most of the differences in costs are related to registration and other fees. By contrast, fees for parent associations and other costs are not too different between the various types of schools. Given higher costs, it is not surprising that FISs in Cameroon serve proportionately more better-off children, with public schools serving proportionately the poor more (secular private schools are even more tilted toward better-off students, as expected). For example, 16 percent of students in faith-inspired schools belong to the poorest quintile of well-being in rural areas, versus 34 percent for government schools. In urban areas, students in the top quintile account for 32 percent of all students in faith-inspired schools, versus 22 percent for public schools.

Thus, while in the Democratic Republic of Congo FISs enroll most students, many of whom are poor, given that close to three fourths of the population is in poverty, in Cameroon FISs serve only a minority of students who are on average better off than the population as a whole. In the case of the Democratic Republic of Congo, FISs tend to have very limited resources, while in the case of Cameroon, through a combination of state subsidies and cost recovery from households who can afford to pay more for schooling, FISs have more resources at their disposal. This brief comparison of the Democratic Republic of Congo and Cameroon is just one example of the heterogeneity that exists between faith-inspired schools in Africa, and there may be a similar degree of heterogeneity within each of the countries, not only according to whom schools serve, how much they cost, and how well they perform but also in terms of the faith traditions to which they belong.

Additional Evidence for Ghana and Burkina Faso

Difference in Benefit Incidence between the Two Surveys for Ghana

In the case of Ghana, there is an issue emerging from the previous section, namely that the two surveys used generate rather different results in terms of the benefit incidence of faith-inspired schools by quintile of well-being. The CWIQ survey suggests a relatively positive outcome for FISs, with the poor benefiting from faith-inspired schools almost as much as other groups, while the GLSS5 suggests that the poor benefit much less than other groups. In theory, this could happen because the two surveys are implemented almost three years apart from each other. Many faith-inspired facilities are located in urban or peri-urban areas, and poverty has been reduced very rapidly in those areas in the first few years of the new millennium. By contrast poverty reduction has been much weaker in rural areas (Coulombe and Wodon 2007). This must have contributed to a deterioration of the benefit incidence in the lower quintiles for education faith-inspired service delivery between the implementation of the CWIQ in 2003 and that of the GLSS5 mostly in 2006.

Apart from the possibility of changes over time in benefit incidence, which of the two surveys is likely to be more appropriate in order to answer the question of whether FISs serve the poor more or less than other groups? Three aspects may be considered to try to answer this question. The first relates to the indicator used to identify the poor in each of the two surveys. In principle, the identification of the poor in the GLSS5 is more precise than in the CWIQ because in the GLSS5, the quintiles of well-being are based on detailed measures of the consumption of household per equivalent adult, while in the CWIQ, the poor are identified through imputed levels of consumption. However, there is a slight problem in the measures of poverty based on the GLSS5 that matters for this study. As discussed by Coulombe and Wodon (2007), because of the use of price indices to update poverty lines over time, and because of a likely underestimation of the increase in the cost of living in urban areas outside of Accra, the estimates of poverty for urban households outside of the capital city are likely to be underestimated in 2005/06. But this is also where a substantial number of FISs are located. Thus the benefit incidence analysis for FISs in the GLSS5 may suggest too few users in the lower quintiles of well-being versus what would be observed otherwise.

The second aspect relates to the sample size of the two surveys. Because the CWIQ survey is much larger than the GLSS5 (49,000 households in the CWIQ versus less than 8,000 in the GLSS5), the number of observations on which the benefit incidence estimates by quintiles are based is also much larger in the CWIQ, which generates a higher level of confidence in those estimates. Overall then, for measuring reach to the poor, the CWIQ survey is probably better than the GLSS5. Also, the surveys were based on a different sampling frame. In terms of the household weights and number of observations in the surveys, it seems that the proportion of the population in urban areas is too high with the GLSS5, and more reasonable with the CWIQ. This also may have contributed to having a better benefit incidence for FISs in the CWIQ than is the case in the GLSS5. Given the above, it is a judgment call as to whether more weight should be placed for the benefit incidence on the CWIQ than on the GLSS5. It is likely that the "right" estimate of benefit incidence is somewhere in between the two estimates provided by the surveys, but possibly closer to the CWIQ results than those obtained with the GLSS5.

Efforts to Reach Vulnerable Groups: Children with Disabilities in Ghana
The evidence presented on Ghana does not mean that FISs do not make efforts to reach the poor and, more generally, vulnerable individuals and households. Even if FISs may not be located more in poor areas, or even if they may not serve the poor statistically more than other groups, or more so than other providers, they may still do what they can to reach the poor and vulnerable within the constraints they face. They may well put in practice a "preferential option for the poor" even if this is not easily detectable from aggregate survey statistics in a simple statistical way. This question will be discussed further in this study, including in chapter 6 when analyzing the cost of services for the poor and the ability of FISs to subsidize the poor. But before doing that, it is useful to document briefly some of the apparent efforts made by FISs to reach the poor and vulnerable.

Consider first the case of children with disabilities in Ghana. The context for this analysis is that historically FISs have had a tradition of support to education beyond the provision of schools. Numerous religious congregations and community organizations support orphans and vulnerable children as well as those in need of special education. This typically gets captured as social work in education rather than as educational service provision. But the first school established in Ghana for those with special needs was set up by missionaries in the 1940s. In the Education Act of 1961 the government assumed responsibility for training and rehabilitation of people with disabilities, but it took some time for this to be translated in practice. The question is whether today, we can observe a difference in terms of attitudes towards children with disabilities between different types of schools, as might be revealed by patterns of enrollment in the various types of schools.

The analysis is carried with the large sample CWIQ survey for 2003. In most household surveys, because the number of children identified as having disabilities is typically small, it is not feasible to conduct detailed statistical or regression analysis to assess whether children with disabilities are less likely to go to school, including by type of school. In the CWIQ survey however, the very large sample size makes such an analysis feasible. The CWIQ survey identifies persons with disabilities, and asks about the type of disability. One question asks about the type of disability according to the following characteristics: Seeing, Hearing/speech, Moving, No feeling, Strange behavior, Fits, Learning, and Other. Because the sample size remains small even in the CWIQ survey according to that categorization, this information is not used. But the survey also asks whether the disability is mild, moderate, or severe, and that information can be used.[4]

Table 5.2 shows that for children aged five to eighteen without disability, the probability of not being enrolled in school is at 21 percent, versus 33 percent for children with one or more disabilities. The likelihood of being enrolled decreases with the severity of the disability. In addition, the data suggest that the likelihood of being enrolled in faith-inspired schools is similar for children with and without disability, while it is lower for children with disabilities in the other two types of schools (public and private secular). It is also clear that in the various types of schools the probability of enrollment decreases with the severity of the disability, but the pattern according to the severity of the disability is less steep for faith-inspired schools. There is thus some statistical evidence that would support the hypothesis that religious schools might be more welcoming to children with disability than other types of schools, although none of the schools are

Table 5.2 Enrollment Rates by Type of Schools and Disability Status, Ghana 2003
percent

	Public	Faith-inspired	Private secular	Not enrolled
Disability status				
No disability	59.4	3.8	15.6	21.1
Disability	48.3	3.9	14.9	32.9
Severity of the disability				
Mild	54.7	3.7	20.3	21.4
Moderate	47.4	4.6	16.4	31.6
Severe	39.9	2.8	4.8	52.5

Source: Estimation based on the Ghana CWIQ 2003. See Adoho and Wodon 2013a.

Table 5.3 **Impact of Disability on School Enrolment by Type of School, Ghana 2003**

	Faith-inspired	Private secular	Not enrolled
Disability	0.0134*	0.0052	0.0351
Moderate disability	−0.0045	0.0031	0.0735**
Severe disability	−0.0029	−0.0647***	0.2675***
Boy	−0.0016	0.0050***	−0.0459***
Boy with a disability	−0.0251**	−0.0057	−0.0074

Source: Estimation based on the Ghana CWIQ 2003. See Adoho and Wodon 2013a.
Note: Statistical significance levels: *=10 percent, **=5 percent, ***=1 percent

particularly good at catering to children with disabilities. In addition, differences between schools may be related to other characteristics of the households sending their children to faith-inspired schools, as opposed to the characteristics of the schools themselves, so that regression analysis is needed to sort this out.

In table 5.3, regression analysis is used to assess whether differences in enrollment patterns between types of schools remain after controlling for household and child characteristics including disability status. The model is a multinomial logit with enrollment in public schools as the reference category (full results are in appendix G). The coefficient estimates for disability and the interaction effect for boys suggest that girls with disabilities are more likely to be enrolled in faith-inspired schools than in public schools, but this is not the case for boys. In fact, boys with a disability are more likely to be enrolled in private secular schools, all other things being equal. However, when a child has a severe disability, the likelihood of enrollment in private secular schools is lower, while there are no differences between faith-inspired and public schools. Of course, the likelihood of not being enrolled is especially high for children that tend to have a more severe disability.

At least two different interpretations can be provided for these results. A first interpretation would be to suggest that the lower likelihood for private schools to enroll students with severe disabilities as compared to both public and religious schools may be due to the fact that private schools tend to be funded independently, and therefore do not have the same obligation as other schools (or the same oversight) to welcome children with a severe disability. Faith-inspired (many of which are publicly funded) and public schools would fare roughly equally because of that legal obligation, or in the case of FISs that are not publicly funded, the acceptance of some children with severe disability might be related to their efforts to serve those who are vulnerable. Another interpretation might be that parents with a child with a severe disability are less likely to send that child to an expensive private school because the expected benefits of schooling for children with disability are lower than for children without disabilities. Under budget constraints, parents would then choose to send in priority children without a disability to private schools. Whatever the explanation, there is some (limited) evidence that faith-inspired schools may make special efforts towards children with severe disabilities, or at least more so than private secular providers.

Conclusion

There is a widespread perception that education FISs in Sub-Saharan Africa reach the poor in priority, yet what this means in practice is often not discussed in detail and with robust empirical evidence. Different interpretations of what "reaching the poor" may mean have been discussed in this chapter. The first interpretation would suggest that FISs serve the poor more than other household groups in their own clientele. Statistically, this seems not to be the case, neither in Sub-Saharan Africa as a whole, nor in Ghana and Burkina Faso. This is not surprising, given that education services are subject to at least some level of cost recovery on the part of FISs as well as other providers, so that the demand for those services is often lower among the poor because of a lack of affordability.

A second interpretation would be to say that FISs serve the poor proportionally more than other providers, and especially public providers (the fact that FISs are likely to serve the poor more than private secular and often for-profit facilities seems clear). The evidence that emerges from nationally representative household surveys is that this is also not necessarily the case. Often, FISs serve the poor about in the same proportion as public providers and in some cases much less so. The evidence on Ghana is mixed. One survey suggests that in Ghana FISs serve the poor about as much as public providers, yielding a similar benefit incidence to that obtained for public facilities. But the other survey suggests that FISs are not well targeted to the poor. While the first survey seems better calibrated than the second, there is no evidence that FISs serve the poor more than public providers, and the same is observed for education in Burkina Faso.

Now, even if FISs may not reach the poor more than other household groups in absolute terms or even in relative terms when compared with public facilities, and even if they are not located proportionately more in poor areas, FISs may still play a special role in making services more affordable for the poor and vulnerable, for example by subsidizing such services in one way or another. They may still, within their means and the constraints they face, try to serve the poor preferentially. In addition, a desire to serve those in need is not necessarily focused only on those who are considered as poor in the traditional monetary sense. In the case of education, one especially vulnerable group is that of children with severe disabilities. Some evidence was provided that FISs make special efforts to welcome children with disabilities in Ghana. As to the question of whether FISs subsidize the poor, it is discussed in the next chapter.

Notes

1. One subquestion here is whether FISs are able to use specific strategies to better serve the poor, for example by cross-subsidizing their services—either within a particular facility, or across a system of facilities. And another sub-question relates to how FISs use their resources. In the case of healthcare for example, Reinikka and Svensson (2010) in a quasi-experiment about the provision of untied block grants to health centers in Uganda that FISs appear not to be motivated by profit or perks maximization, but rather by a desire to make more of their services available and affordable to the poor—that is, they seem to be "working for God."

2. As mentioned in chapter 2, depending on the survey, the quintiles are based either on measures of consumption per capita or per equivalent adult taking into account differences in the cost of living between areas, or on an index of wealth obtained using factorial analysis when consumption data is not available.
3. Performance, as measured by perceptions among parents as to whether their children can read and write in English or French (Cameroon is a bilingual country), suggests that faith-inspired schools may do slightly less well than other schools in urban areas, but better in rural areas (this is based on simple statistics however, and not on econometric analysis controlling for a range of factors that may affect performance).
4. Rates of disability as measured in household surveys such as the CWIQ tend to be underestimated, with estimates of the population with a disability typically in the range of two to three percent, while it has been suggested based on other more detailed data that also captures less severe forms of disability that the proportion of people with disabilities might be much higher, at up to ten percent in many countries. Yet, for the point of view of the analysis carried here, even if the incidence of disability is indeed underestimated, one can still measure differences in enrollment by school types between those declaring a disability in the survey.

CHAPTER 6

Private Cost of Education

Introduction

The questions of the extent to which faith-inspired schools (FISs) reach the poor is closely related to the cost for households of the services provided by FISs in comparison to other providers, and the amount of funding available to FISs. In some cases, FISs may benefit from special resources to make services more affordable for the poor, for example when they get support from congregations, whether these are locally based or located in developed countries, or from other organizations including government agencies. In the absence of such support, subsidies granted to the poor may require charging better-off students more for the services provided to those groups, or relying on staffs who are willing to work at below market wages.

Different strategies for reducing the cost of services for the poor may not have the same medium- or long-term consequences. For example, relying on staffs who are willing to work at below market wages (as may be the case for nuns), or on resources made available by external groups may not carry a risk in terms of financial sustainability as long as the staffs are willing to continue to work for low wages or as long as external funders are willing to continue to provide resources in order to make services more affordable for the poor.

By contrast, differentiated subsidies for the poor paid for by asking higher fees from other groups—what could be referred to as a Robin Hood strategy—would not be sustainable under competitive markets. Indeed, under competitive markets, subsidies for the poor would lead not only to poor students relying on FISs as compared to other facilities but also to fewer nonpoor students, which would ultimately be unsustainable in the absence of other funding or cost reduction mechanisms, such as those mentioned earlier. It might be feasible under different types of markets to charge more to the better-off in order to subsidize the poor— for example, under a segmented market with quality differentiated among others according to faith, better-off households who value the faith affiliation of a school may be willing to pay more for that school than for another school, which may then make it feasible for a facility to subsidize the services provided to the poor.

Yet it is not clear how much resources might be generated through price differentiation for such purposes.

The fact that the issues of cost and funding go hand in hand is exemplified by an interesting analysis of health service provision in Uganda by Reinikka and Svensson (2010). The authors use a change in financing of not-for-profit healthcare providers through untied grants to test two theories of organizational behaviour. The first theory postulates that not-for-profit providers are intrinsically motivated to serve the poor and will therefore use new resources to expand their services or cut the cost of these services. The second theory postulates that not-for-profit providers are captured by their managers or workers and behave like for-profit actors. Although they may not appropriate profits, they would tend to use untied grants to raise the salaries of their staff or provide them with other benefits that would not directly serve the poor. The authors' empirical results suggest that the altruistic theory is validated by the data (the grants were used to provide more services at lower costs), and that the results matter in the sense that this altruistic difference makes a difference for the poor.

Household surveys can be used to test for differences in the cost of education between facilities, and between different types of households depending on their level of well-being. This can be done after controlling for a range of factors that may affect the cost or education for households, as well as for the endogeneity of provider choice on the part of households. This is done in this chapter together with cross-country evidence on the cost of FISs in section 2, followed as usual by a more detailed analysis for Ghana and Burkina Faso in section 3.

Cross-Country Evidence

Many but not all of the multipurpose household surveys used for this study have information on the cost paid by households for education. Summary statistics for the average costs by type of provider are provided in tables 6.1 and 6.2 for nine countries where that information is available. These are yearly costs for primary and secondary schooling. These are not the total costs paid by households—for example transport costs are not included, nor are costs for uniforms and textbooks for examples, but these are the costs paid to schools for the services received. On the other hand, apart from fees, PTA (Parent-Teacher Associations) dues are also included, as these tend to fund operating expenses. All costs have been presented in US dollars, using the exchange rates at the time of the surveys.

There is a clear ranking in costs between the various types of providers. For both primary and secondary schooling, in all but one country (Sierra Leone), public schools are cheaper than faith-inspired schools (in Swaziland, there is a virtual tie). As for other private schools, they are more expensive than both public and faith-inspired schools in all nine countries at the primary level, and in all but one country (Cameroon) at the secondary level. One should of course be careful about simple statistical comparisons, in that the reasons for differences in costs may be many. A more detailed analysis for Ghana and Burkina Faso of the private costs of primary education will be provided below. Still, it appears that

Table 6.1 Cost of School Fees and PTA Dues in Primary Schools
US$

	Residence area		Welfare quintile					
	Urban	Rural	Q1	Q2	Q3	Q4	Q5	Total
	Burundi, 2006							
Public	2.5	1.5	1.3	1.5	1.5	1.4	2.2	1.5
Faith-inspired	0.3	2.0	4.3	0.9	0.8	1.4	0.7	1.9
Private secular	41.7	2.7	0.4	0.3	2.8	9.3	41.7	24.4
Total	8.3	1.5	1.4	1.5	1.5	1.4	4.8	1.9
	Cameroon, 2007							
Public	13.5	7.7	6.5	7.6	9.5	11.4	16.3	9.1
Faith-inspired	54.0	23.2	17.7	25.1	29.8	41.8	58.6	35.3
Private secular	108.4	44.0	22.1	43.9	63.2	80.0	139.0	98.3
Total	50.5	10.7	7.5	11.5	18.2	29.4	71.7	24.2
	Ghana, 2005/06							
Public	7.6	1.7	1.3	2.3	2.8	4.6	10.1	3.3
Faith-inspired	41.5	13.7	3.0	13.0	19.1	31.9	50.2	30.2
Private secular	56.2	19.7	20.0	28.3	31.7	40.6	63.7	41.9
Total	27.8	4.4	2.7	5.9	9.2	17.5	36.0	12.7
	Sierra Leone, 2003/04							
Public	3.7	1.7	1.6	1.7	2.1	2.5	5.3	2.7
Faith-inspired	2.9	1.3	1.1	1.5	2.0	2.1	3.6	1.9
Private secular	41.4	2.2	1.8	2.2	17.7	19.3	36.2	16.9
Total	6.0	1.5	1.3	1.6	2.6	3.5	8.9	3.3
	Swaziland, 2009/10							
Public	73.0	22.4	13.8	20.2	20.5	38.7	66.0	26.8
Faith-inspired	78.5	27.4	11.1	23.7	29.0	30.2	103.3	31.4
Private secular	409.7	122.9	20.2	51.6	69.1	98.8	439.8	218.5
Total	167.9	30.4	13.3	22.6	25.4	43.5	172.9	44.9
	Kenya, 2005							
Public	7.9	1.9	0.8	1.1	2.2	3.3	8.6	2.6
Faith-inspired	79.1	57.1	17.8	19.8	32.3	63.9	119.0	65.9
Private secular	128.8	72.3	15.3	33.9	58.8	71.5	149.2	97.4
Total	39.4	6.2	1.3	2.6	5.2	11.7	45.8	11.1
	Malawi, 2004							
Public	0.4	0	0	0	0.1	0.1	0.3	0.1
Faith-inspired	11.0	0.1	0	0.1	0.2	0.1	5.9	0.9
Private secular	107.4	9.6	0.2	1.2	8.3	8.0	103.9	72.0
Total	13.0	0.1	0	0.1	0.1	0.2	9.9	1.6

table continues next page

Table 6.1 Cost of School Fees and PTA Dues in Primary Schools *(continued)*
US$

	Residence area		Welfare quintile					
	Urban	Rural	Q1	Q2	Q3	Q4	Q5	Total
			Nigeria 2003/04					
Public	10.2	3.9	4.0	2.8	3.7	8.1	13.5	6.6
Faith-inspired	15.6	5.1	4.1	16.0	3.6	15.9	14.7	11.4
Private secular	46.4	14.5	33.0	30.2	25.6	28.6	55.5	39.4
Total	21.7	4.8	7.8	7.6	6.8	12.5	27.7	13.4
			Uganda, 2010					
Public	19.2	3.7	2.0	2.5	3.7	5.6	19.7	4.8
Faith-inspired	71.7	22.1	5.3	9.6	19.7	36.9	75.5	31.4
Private secular	124.8	44.5	16.4	22.6	31.2	47.5	119.9	63.2
Total	71.2	11.4	3.1	5.4	9.4	17.2	70.6	17.6
			Average					
Public	17.2	5.6	3.9	5.0	5.8	9.5	17.7	7.2
Faith-inspired	44.3	19.0	8.0	13.7	17.0	28.0	53.9	26.3
Private secular	133.1	41.6	16.2	26.8	38.6	50.5	143.6	84.0
Total	50.7	8.9	4.8	7.4	9.8	17.1	56.0	16.3

Source: Estimation from the various countries' surveys. See Tsimpo and Wodon 2013b.

Table 6.2 Cost of School Fees and PTA Dues in Secondary Schools
US$

	Residence area		Welfare quintile					
	Urban	Rural	Q1	Q2	Q3	Q4	Q5	Total
			Burundi, 2006					
Public	15.0	9.7	9.8	11.1	8.3	10.9	11.8	10.4
Faith-inspired	71.7	9.6	18.7	10.0	5.1	1.2	44.8	22.3
Private secular	48.2	25.5	20.4	9.7	26.4	25.0	49.8	42.3
Total	31.8	10.4	10.5	11.0	9.4	12.0	23.9	15.0
			Cameroon, 2007					
Public	46.9	37.4	33.2	36.4	39.6	42.3	49.9	41.5
Faith-inspired	184.2	142.1	137.4	98.0	135.9	167.5	219.3	175.1
Private secular	166.1	114.2	86.2	127.4	134.8	157.5	180.7	160.5
Total	98.4	44.1	36.7	47.3	60.6	77.3	104.7	73.9
			Ghana, 2005/06					
Public	42.0	13.7	8.0	10.2	28.2	31.6	53.1	26.9
Faith-inspired	69.0	55.3	84.6	51.9	44.8	56.7	85.0	64.8
Private secular	94.4	52.3	48.2	49.4	70.8	68.1	116.0	80.1
Total	54.9	19.5	12.7	16.8	34.0	40.3	71.1	37.6

table continues next page

Table 6.2 Cost of School Fees and PTA Dues in Secondary Schools *(continued)*
US$

	Residence area		Welfare quintile					Total
	Urban	Rural	Q1	Q2	Q3	Q4	Q5	
			Sierra Leone, 2003/04					
Public	15.9	11.3	14.2	10.2	14.9	14.3	15.4	14.6
Faith-inspired	15.0	7.6	9.4	11.4	12.0	12.9	14.6	12.6
Private secular	28.1	4.6	14.2	40.3	25.5	9.8	22.1	22.6
Total	16.0	9.5	11.3	11.7	13.6	13.6	15.6	14.1
			Swaziland, 2009/10					
Public	189.7	103.1	31.8	68.6	88.8	143.5	258.4	114.1
Faith-inspired	212.8	94.1	9.9	57.8	60.7	148.6	220.3	112.6
Private secular	560.0	598.6	15.7	0	309.6	217.9	793.7	580.9
Total	264.7	121.7	26.9	66.5	95.5	146.7	359.9	143.9
			Kenya, 2005					
Public	147.8	92.6	50.2	75.1	93.4	105.5	136.9	101.7
Faith-inspired	109.9	109.5	133.7	83.9	84.2	92.0	150.8	109.6
Private secular	138.3	117.4	41.8	96.0	91.6	112.2	176.5	127.4
Total	141.3	95.6	53.0	77.9	92.5	105.1	145.0	105.4
			Malawi, 2004					
Public	29.6	14.1	11.0	15.8	14.3	16.4	22.8	17.7
Faith-inspired	93.1	14.5	37.8	45.0	22.3	17.8	68.1	51.3
Private secular	115.3	26.5	10.3	20.4	28.7	30.7	97.9	67.6
Total	66.9	16.3	12.4	16.8	17.0	19.1	51.4	31.5
			Nigeria 2003/04					
Public	23.6	19.5	9.4	14.9	16.4	22.5	32.9	21.6
Faith-inspired	52.5	21.6	20.5	24.0	12.9	41.9	70.8	44.3
Private secular	96.8	26.2	21.0	24.3	43.6	72.8	105.2	75.2
Total	38.0	20.2	10.7	15.8	19.5	30.3	48.7	29.8
			Uganda, 2010					
Public	160.8	73.3	36.7	41.3	53.8	91.3	181.5	88.6
Faith-inspired	274.8	131.6	57.6	126.9	43.0	188.2	257.9	162.8
Private secular	229.2	169.9	53.6	97.2	109.4	139.3	270.0	190.3
Total	207.6	115.6	42.4	61.2	72.9	115.2	241.1	139.1
			Average					
Public	83.9	46.9	25.5	35.5	44.7	59.8	95.3	54.6
Faith-inspired	135.4	73.2	63.7	63.6	52.6	90.9	141.5	94.4
Private secular	184.5	141.9	38.9	58.1	105.1	104.2	226.5	168.4
Total	114.9	56.6	27.1	40.6	51.9	70.0	132.7	73.8

Source: Estimation from the various countries' surveys. See Tsimpo and Wodon 2013b.

there are substantial differences in costs between FISs, private secular, and public providers in many of the countries.

A few more comments are warranted for tables 6.1 and 6.2. First, there are large differences in costs between areas. Costs are higher in urban than in rural areas. Second, costs are higher for those in the top quintiles as compared to lower quintiles. This is not surprising, given that the costs paid are influenced by the ability to pay of households—wealthier households will tend to put their children in better and more expensive schools. Whether the poor pay less for what could be referred to as similar schooling, or at least for similar households, is however a question that requires more analysis than what is presented in tables 6.1 and 6.2, as will be discussed for Ghana and Burkina Faso in the next section.

Additional Evidence for Ghana and Burkina Faso

Comparative Cost of Faith-Inspired Education for Households in Ghana

In the case of Ghana, the evidence presented in section 3.1. suggests that the cost of education in FISs is higher than that in public facilities. This section looks in more details at the cost of primary schools in Ghana. Table 6.3 provides basic statistics on the private cost of primary schooling for parents in the GLSS5. FISs are on average almost twice as expensive as public schools and private schools are even more expensive. This would suggest that the poor are not very likely to attend faith-inspired schools, at least in the GLSS5 sample, and this is confirmed by the benefit incidence analysis in chapter 5 [see, however, the discussion comparing the Core Welfare Indicators Questionnaire (CWIQ) and Ghana Living Standard Survey, Fifth Round (GLSS5) surveys in that chapter]. When considering only the school and registration fees, as well as contributions to PTAs, the differences are even larger proportionately. Yet average costs do not control for a wide range of factors that could affect out-of-pocket expenditures.

Table 6.3 Cost of Primary Education by Type of School, Divided by 10,000, 2005/06 (GHC)

Types of school	School and registration fees	Contribution to PTAs	Uniform and sport clothes	Books and school supplies	Transportation to and from School
Public	14.2	1.0	4.5	7.6	4.0
Faith-inspired	41.3	1.7	6.7	13.4	10.9
Private secular	56.9	1.7	7.0	14.8	15.6
All	22.6	1.1	5.0	9.1	6.3

Types of school	Foods, boards and lodging at school	Expenses on extra classes	In-kind expenses	Other expenses & no breakdown	Total expense
Public	31.2	4.1	0.4	17.1	83.9
Faith-inspired	47.9	8.7	0.7	29.3	160.7
Private secular	49.5	13.5	1.0	51.5	211.3
All	35.2	5.8	0.5	23.3	108.9

Sources: Estimation based on GLSS5. See Adoho and Wodon 2013b. Amounts divided by 10,000.

Even if faith-inspired primary schools are more expensive for households than public schools in Ghana, is it the case that they try to make their services affordable to at least some of the poor? In order to try to measure the cost of education for various types of households, regression analysis is used. The costs being considered include school fees and registration fees, contribution to parent/teachers associations, and expenses on extra classes received by the schools. The regressors are (1) the type of school attended by the child (this variable is instrumented as explained below); (2) the grade in school that the child is attending (with the first grade of the cycle being the reference category); (3) characteristics of the child—the age of the child, whether s/he is the oldest child in the household, and whether s/he lives with his or her biological family; (4) the geographic location of the child according to urban or rural status and the main areas in the country (with Accra as reference category); (5) the quintile of consumption per equivalent adult of the household in which the child lives together with interaction effects with the type of school attended; (6) whether the household head is male or female, and his/her age; and (7) the education level of the household head.

As mentioned in chapter 3, there is concern that the choice of provider may be endogenous, that is it may depend itself on the cost of schooling. To avoid endogeneity bias the choice of provider is instrumented through a separate multinomial logit regression that assesses the probability of seeking a specific provider as a function of the same set of controls, plus the faith of the individual (faith may lead some to seek FISs, but this should not influence cost after such decision is made), and the leave-out-mean probability that individuals located in the same primary sampling unit (PSU) or area as the household choose one or another type of provider. This last variable measures neighborhood availability and quality or value effects—the more likely it is that other households rely on one specific type of school in a geographic area, the more likely it is that the individual will also rely on those schools, but this again should not influence cost for the individual after the decision of choosing a specific type of school has been made. This strategy of identifying the outcome regression through a leave-out mean PSU-level variable affecting the choice of facility by individuals was used by Ravallion and Wodon (2000) in work on schooling and child labor in Bangladesh and by Wodon (2000) in work on the impact of low-income energy policies on the probability of electricity disconnection in France.

Key results from the second-stage tobit regression on the cost of education are shown in table 6.4 (the full regression results are in appendix G, and bootstrapping is used to correct standard errors for the two-stage procedure). It appears that there are no differences in costs between public and faith-inspired facilities once controls are introduced. Private facilities are however more expensive, as expected, and with few differences by quintile, given that the quintile effects and the interacted effects with private providers tend to offset each others.

An important finding in table 6.4 is that there is a clear differentiation in costs paid by quintiles of well-being, with households from higher quintiles paying more than households from lower quintiles, especially in faith-inspired and public facilities (given the counteracting interaction effects for private facilities). This

Table 6.4 Selected Correlates of the Cost of Education, Ghana, 2005/06

Variables	Coefficient	t-stats
Provider (instrumented)		
Private secular	4.90***	3.388
Faith-inspired	−6.60	−0.865
Level of well-being		
Quintile 2	0.21	0.967
Quintile 3	0.41*	1.789
Quintile 4	0.68***	2.760
Quintile 5	1.25***	4.129
Interaction effects		
Private secular x Quintile 2	−1.50	−0.993
Private secular x Quintile 3	−1.77	−1.215
Private secular x Quintile 4	−2.56*	−1.774
Private secular x Quintile 5	−3.46**	−2.392
Faith-inspired x Quintile 2	6.04	0.851
Faith-inspired x Quintile 3	5.79	0.749
Faith-inspired x Quintile 4	8.35	1.099
Faith-inspired x Quintile 5	8.35	1.090

Sources: Estimation based on GLSS5. See Adoho and Wodon 2013b.
Note: Statistical significance levels: *=10 percent, **=5 percent, ***=1 percent.

pattern could in principle be consistent with a Robin Hood pricing hypothesis in faith-inspired schools whereby differentiated subsidies for the poor would be paid for by asking higher fees from other groups. Such a pricing strategy would probably not be sustainable under competitive markets, since subsidies for the poor would lead not only to poor students relying on FISs as compared to other facilities but also to fewer nonpoor students, which would ultimately be unsustainable in the absence of other funding or cost reduction mechanisms. But in a segmented market with different types of schools providing different types of services, it might be sustainable, as better-off households that value the faith affiliation of a school may be willing to pay more for that school than for another school. At the same time, the results in table 6.4 are also consistent with a simpler hypothesis whereby better-off households might simply select schools that are more expensive and provide better quality, or may be located in areas where the overall cost of schools is higher in general, and the fact that there are no differences between faith-inspired and public schools would not tend to specifically favor the Robin Hood pricing strategy hypothesis.

Cost, School Inputs, and Performance of Education Services in Burkina Faso

Consider now education costs in Burkina Faso. Results from the 2007 QUIBB survey in table 6.5 suggest that more than one in four children aged 7–12 not in primary school are not attending due to the financial burden that schooling represents (many fees were abolished in 2007, but this may not be reflected yet in the survey). After the reason that school is "not necessary" which may indicate a lack of quality in schooling or a lack of jobs despite better schooling, cost was the second main reason given for nonattendance. The percentages are the same for rural and urban children and are fairly consistent across economic groups, though lower for the wealthiest as expected (the large proportion of parents mentioning "not of school age" is due to late entry practiced for a nonnegligible share of children; note that the statistics in table 6.5 are computed among those not enrolled in school).

The qualitative fieldwork conducted in a few areas confirms that despite the reforms implemented in 2007, the cost of schooling remains a constraint for some families in Burkina Faso. A significant number of respondents listed the cost of education as a disadvantage of their school (23.3 percent in public schools, 35.5 percent in Franco-Arab schools, and 20 percent in Christian schools). The smaller share in Christian schools probably reflects the larger average incomes of respondents sending their children to those schools. When asked in a separate question if they were satisfied with the level of the fees at their school, while 83.3 percent of Christian school parents said that they were very satisfied or satisfied, the proportion was only 42.0 percent for parents at Islamic schools. Table 6.6 provides

Table 6.5 Reason for Not Attending School in Burkina Faso, Children Aged 7–12 (FCFA)
percent

	Residence area		Welfare quintiles					
	Urban	Rural	Q1 (poorest)	Q2	Q3	Q4	Q5 (richest)	Total
Failed exam	4.0	1.3	1.0	0.9	2.1	1.4	2.5	1.4
Completed school	0	0.1	0	0	0	0.4	0	0.1
Working	1.2	2.4	1.8	2.9	2.9	1.4	1.8	2.4
Too expensive	27.4	27.1	24.6	29.4	30.8	28.0	19.9	27.2
Not necessary, refused	36.1	29.6	24.6	29.5	29.9	34.1	42.4	29.8
Too far away	3.6	12.4	20.5	8.3	9.5	6.8	7.1	12.1
No canteen	0	0.3	0.4	0	0	0.1	0	0.3
Illness	6.2	1.6	0.8	2.3	2.3	1.8	3.7	1.7
Marriage/pregnancy	0.4	0.1	0	0	0	0	0.6	0.1
Not of school age	21.1	25.3	26.3	26.3	22.4	26.0	21.9	25.1
All	100.0	100.0	100.0	100.0	100.0	100.0	100.0	100.0

Source: Estimation based on QUIBB 2007.

Table 6.6 Average Annual School Expenses per Child, Burkina Faso Fieldwork

	Islamic schools	Christian schools	Public schools
School fees	Rural: 8,000 Urban: 15,000–30,000	Protestant: Rural: 8,000; Urban: 15,000–30,000 Catholic: Rural: 30,000; Urban: 35,000	—
Uniforms	2,204	4,433	1,385
Transportation	0	4,545	0
Books and supplies	5,648	16,350	2,708

Source: Burkina Faso fieldwork. See Gemignani and Wodon 2013.

data on the costs for parents to send their children to the various types of schools represented in the fieldwork. School fees in the Catholic schools are set at about 30,000 FCFA in rural areas and 35,000 FCFA in urban areas. Fees at the other faith-inspired schools vary significantly. The rural schools had much lower fees at about 7,500 FCFA to 9,000 FCFA for both Islamic and Christian schools, but the urban schools charged between 16,000 FCFA and 40,000 FCFA. In addition, parents have to pay additional costs for uniforms, transportation, and books and supplies.

Almost 40 percent of parents in the Islamic schools stated that a major disadvantage faced by their schools was the parents' inability to pay school fees, and they linked this inability to lower salaries of teachers and subsequent quality issues. They also stated that when children leave the Islamic schools, this is most often for economic reasons. Indeed the most common reason given for boys leaving a school was financial difficulties (48.4 percent of those leaving). Results were similar for public schools with 46.7 percent of parents saying that boys leave school due to financial hardship (in the case of girls, the figures were lower, with 40 percent of parents in Muslim and public schools citing marriage as the main reason leading girls to end their schooling.) In their evaluation of the problems faced by their schools, several parents as well as school administrators stated that although they felt that Franco-Arab schools have benefitted the community, parents were having ongoing problems in caring for the basic needs of children who attended the school, including affording clothing, food, medical needs, and especially school fees. As the director of a Franco-Arab school stated: "These children come from underprivileged situations where the majority of parents are illiterate and poor. They are not able to nourish them, look after them, and to suitably provide education for them and this is often the source of school abandonment." Over a third of parents in these schools suggest that there is a need to lower school fees to a level that parents would be able to afford, so that children may continue their education.

School officials are well aware of the fact that parents in Franco-Arab schools often do not pay the required amount of school fees. In addition to the financial difficulties faced by parents, they suggested that another contributing factor may be the popular conception, linked to the history of Islamic schooling, that an Islamic education should be provided free or at very low cost to the Muslim community. One parent stated that some community members "see only the religious teaching, as in the Qur'anic schools, and their contributions to equip the school with resources are tiny in spite of the sensitizing efforts of the founder."

Catholic schools are in a different position because their clientele tends to be better off. This makes it feasible for the schools to provide education opportunities to some of those in need. But in order to finance the schools, the fees are set quite high and are not affordable by the poor in Burkina Faso, except the few that may be subsidized. It is because wealthier families are willing to pay for the quality of the education received that the Catholic schools may provide assistance to some families that cannot afford their school fees. The difference between Catholic and Islamic schools appears as well in the data from the Ministry of

Table 6.7 School Inputs by Type of School, Burkina Faso 2008/09
percent

	Private Secular	Private Catholic	Private Islamic	Private Protestant	Public schools
	Teacher qualifications				
Teaching assistant	67.3	13.8	32.4	67.7	0.3
Qualified teaching asst.	21.6	57.0	1.4	20.5	51.0
Qualified teacher	9.4	28.4	0.3	11.0	47.4
Head teacher	0.7	0.4	0	0	0.2
Other/missing	0.9	0.4	65.9	0.8	1.1
Total	100	100	100	100	100
	School facilities				
Canteen	25.8	59.7	31.8	45.4	75.9
Potable water	70.1	67.9	16.5	63.2	46.5
Electricity	53.8	47.0	7.2	41.4	9.1
Toilets	87.5	85.1	32.2	80.9	68.2
	Number of manuals and textbooks per child				
Math	0.53	0.59	0.21	0.53	0.77
Geography.	0.34	0.45	0.11	0.34	0.53
History	0.42	0.50	0.14	0.42	0.59
Reading	0.83	0.91	0.48	0.91	1.25
Natural science	0.50	0.59	0.18	0.50	0.71

Source: Ministry of Education of Burkina Faso.

Education on the characteristics of the schools (table 6.7). Teachers in public and Catholic schools have on average the highest levels of qualification. For example, the Instituteur Adjoint Certifié (IAC) or Instituteur Certifié (IC) certification is held by 98.4 percent of teachers in public schools and 85.4 percent in Catholic schools. The ability of Catholic schools to attract qualified teachers may be related to the fact that they receive state assistance for teacher salaries. By contrast only 31.5 percent of teachers in Protestant schools have the IAC or IC teaching credentials, with 67 percent of the teachers in those schools listed as teaching assistants (Instituteur Adjoint [IA] level). Teachers in Islamic schools have even lower rates of formal training with only 1.7 percent having the IAC or IC level, 32.4 percent the IA level, and 62.8 percent other credentials (possibly a college degree but also a high school diploma).

Table 6.7 suggests fewer systematic differences between public, Catholic, and Protestant schools in school amenities. Public schools are more likely to have a canteen (75.9 percent compared to 59.7 percent in Catholic and 45.4 percent in Protestant schools). But drinking water is more often available in Catholic and Protestant schools (67.9 percent and 63.2 percent respectively, as compared to 46.5 percent in public schools) as are toilet facilities (85.1 percent and 80.9 percent, as compared to 68.2 percent in public schools). The largest difference here is the fact that only 9.1 percent of public schools have access to electricity, as compared to 47.0 percent and 41.4 percent respectively for

Catholic and Protestant schools. This likely indicates neighborhood effects, with Catholic and Protestant schools more likely to be located in urban and wealthier areas than in rural areas. Islamic schools are the worst off in terms of basic amenities, with less than a third of the schools having canteens and toilets, 16.5 percent having drinking water, and 7.2 percent electricity.

Islamic schools also have a smaller number of textbooks and teaching manuals per students than other schools. By contrast Catholic, Protestant, and secular private schools have similar textbook/student ratios, and public schools tend to do best. For mathematics for example, there are almost five children per book in the Islamic schools as compared to two children per boom in the other types of schools. On the other hand Islamic schools tend to have lower student/teacher ratios (25 students per teacher in Islamic schools, compared to 46 in Catholic schools and 50 in Protestant and public schools), which may reflect the fact that some of the schools may be located in poorer and more isolated areas. Thus, while Islamic schools employ teachers that tend to have lower certifications, they employ more of them per student.

Conversations in the qualitative fieldwork with school administrators and government officials suggested the need for better trained staff in Islamic schools. They pointed out that the salaries of teachers in Islamic schools are low in comparison to those in public and Catholic schools. Discussions with school leaders confirmed this, with Islamic teaching staff in the three schools earning around 25,000 FCFA per month, compared to 95,000–125,000 FCFA in public and Catholic schools. While Islamic school teachers sometimes benefit from room and board, their total compensation remains low. By contrast, a director at a Catholic school described the large investments made in teacher quality in the school and felt that this was the reason for higher student achievement in the school. Beyond teacher training, the school also maintained a system for regular monitoring of teacher quality made possible thanks to the resources of the school.

Statistics on student achievement are available for the Catholic school system. These show that 81.3 percent of Catholic primary school students passed the Certificat d'Etudes Primaires (CEP) examination in 2009, compared to 58.4 percent for Burkina Faso overall. Similar statistics on test scores in Islamic schools are however not available. A very small number of Islamic schools (six) were included in the 2009 PASEC study which reports a negative correlation between Islamic schools and test scores. Results from the qualitative fieldwork suggest however a great deal of variability in test scores between Islamic schools. At one of the Franco-Arab schools visited, 88.5 percent of students had passed the CEP examination, comparing favorably with the national average and surpassing the average for the Catholic schools. This school was well known for the academic success of its students. At a second large Franco-Arab school, the CEP pass rate was however only 30 percent, and as low as 18.8 percent for girls.

Finally, data on student passing rates by type of school are also available and provided in table 6.8 by grades. Except for a lower Catholic CM1 passing rate, the passing rates for Catholic and secular private schools are consistently higher

Table 6.8 Passing Rate in Primary Schools by Grade, Burkina Faso 2008/09
percent

Measure	Private Secular	Private Catholic	Private Islamic	Private Protestant	Public
Pass Rate CP1	87.2	88.6	73.0	85.1	86.8
Pass Rate CP2	96.6	94.7	71.5	87.6	87.3
Pass Rate CE1	86.0	88.2	64.5	80.7	82.6
Pass Rate CE2	92.7	94.7	64.3	87.2	83.7
Pass Rate CM1	86.9	75.2	61.1	73.7	73.6

Source: Ministry of Education of Burkina Faso.

than for other schools. Protestant and public schools have similar passing rates, while Islamic schools have lower passing rates. While passing rates are not necessarily measures of performance, the information provided by passing rates together with other data tend to suggest better performance in Catholic and private secular schools than in public and Protestant schools, with Islamic schools lagging somewhat behind. However, because this information does not take into account any information on the characteristics of the student population (Islamic schools tend to welcome poorer students, as mentioned previously), this is not necessarily indicative of the performance of the schools themselves. But the fact that both student attainment and achievement tend to be higher in Catholic schools helps in explaining why they are able to attract students from wealthier background.

Conclusion

Cross-country evidence suggests a clear ranking in the private costs of education between the various types of providers for both primary and secondary schooling. In most countries, public schools tend to be cheaper on average, followed by FISs, and then private secular schools. At the same time, there is also substantial diversity today in how FISs provide education services in African countries, and whom they serve, and this is also observed in Ghana and Burkina Faso. FISs often aim to serve all—but many also have a commitment to serve the poor and vulnerable. The extent to which they are actually able to do so (given their resources) remains an open question. Even if FISs do benefit from staffs who are dedicated, some of whom may be able and willing to work for very low pay, running a school does cost money, and financial sustainability requires funding. When FISs do not benefit from state support, or when they benefit from lower levels of state support than public facilities, they need to rely on cost recovery from students to break even. When higher cost recovery is required from users, it is more difficult for FISs to serve the poor, because the cost of their services becomes less affordable for those in need.

Once household characteristics are taken into account, econometric analysis carried for Ghana suggests no clear differentiation in costs between faith-inspired and public schools, but better-off households do tend to pay more than the very poor even after a range of controls are accounted for. This could be in principle consistent with Robin Hood pricing on the part of FISs, but also with other explanations, including that better-off households simply purchase better services, or live in areas where the services are pricier. In Burkina Faso, there is some evidence than Christian schools, and especially Catholic schools, may on average serve the better-off more, even if they do make some efforts to make their services available to some among the poor. These schools also tend to have better student attainment and achievement results. By contrast, many Islamic schools tend to serve children who are poor, which is not too surprising, given that Muslim populations are indeed poorer (in both countries). When they are unable or unwilling to raise fees, the quality of at least some of the faith-inspired schools may be lower than it would be otherwise, with teachers being paid significantly less in Islamic schools, as compared to public and Catholic schools. But these Islamic schools still provide value for parents—indeed, as discussed in the next chapter, a key reason for parents to send their children to faith-inspired schools is the fact that the schools, and especially Islamic school, integrate religion education in their curriculum. This emphasis placed on religion, and more generally on values and morality, is important for many parents, and this is the topic of focus in the next chapter.

CHAPTER 7

Satisfaction and Preferences

Introduction

In the previous three chapters, the focus was in large part on the supply side of faith-inspired service delivery, since the market, share reach to the poor, and cost of faith-inspired schools (FISs) depend in large part on decisions made by the staffs and managers of FISs, even if they also represent some form of equilibrium between supply and demand in each of the local markets in which FISs operate. With this last chapter, the focus shifts more to the demand side of service delivery, with a discussion of the satisfaction of households with the services they receive, and the reasons that lead them to rely on faith-inspired facilities.

The perception in the literature is that FISs have a comparative advantage, or that they provide special values through their services, in part because of their commitment to quality as well as serving the poor, both of which are made feasible through the dedication of their staffs. Even with limited resources, FISs may be able to provide services of quality, including to the poor. Still, as was the case for questions related to market share, reach to the poor, and cost, systematic evidence on the comparative advantages of FISs and satisfaction with their services remains thin. Measuring satisfaction is not easy as analysis based on exit interviews or national surveys suffers from self-selection bias since students/parents who choose to go to a particular facility are more likely to be satisfied with that facility. Much of the analysis presented in this section also suffers from this selection bias. Beyond the measurement of satisfaction rates, many other questions remain unanswered. For example, making the link with the previous chapter on cost and funding, if students/parents are more satisfied with FISs, is this because of lower costs or despite higher costs? Answers to such questions are likely to be country- and context-specific.

The specific case of education is especially complex, given the differences between various types of schools, and especially Islamic schools. Islamic schools are perhaps not simply FISs providing services like any other organization. They are distinct from an Islamic point of view from other schools. As noted by Sikand (2005, 2008a, 2008b, 2009) in the case of South Asia, if the main objective of *madrasas* remains that of providing a religious education to future Islamic scholars (with an emphasis on religious knowledge that is stronger than what is found in Christian schools), this should be one of the yardsticks according to which their performance should be evaluated. In this respect, *madrasas* may actually perform rather well. This implies that *madrasas* are not simply one player in a larger education services marketplace. One could probably argue that becoming just one such player is precisely what some *madrasa* leaders would like to avoid, and why they resist calls for reforms to include more secular topics in the curriculum, since adopting such reforms could make their services less distinct and thus potentially less appealing to those who do want an Islamic educational environment for their children. The situation is slightly different in Sub-Saharan Africa, but it is clear that faith is a key reason for households to choose faith-inspired schools.

Another difficulty is the distinction between satisfaction and performance. In order to improve human development outcomes, performance is what matters ultimately, and more so than satisfaction per se, even if both are likely to be correlated. Performance also tends to be more objective, while satisfaction is more subjective. There is some evidence in the education literature that faith-inspired providers may offer services of higher or equal quality to those provided by public schools (for example, Allcott and Ortega 2009; Asadullah et al. 2009; Altonji et al. 2005; Cox and Jimenez 1990; Evans and Schwab 1995; González and Arévalo 2005; Hoxby 1994; Hsieh and Urquiola 2006; Parra Osorio and Wodon 2011). In Sub-Saharan Africa, Wodon and Ying (2009) find that in Sierra Leone faith-inspired schools perform slightly better than public schools after controls are taken into account for the type of students enrolled, while Backiny-Yetna and Wodon (2009b) find similar performance between faith-inspired and public schools in the Democratic Republic of Congo.

Discussing the satisfaction of users with services, as well as the reasons for choosing FISs and their performance, is a tall order. The emphasis in this chapter will be more on satisfaction and the reasons for choosing FISs or preferences, as opposed to performance. Only one brief case study on the performance of Ghana's schools will be provided, based on the literacy and numeracy of students as perceived by parents. Because an understanding of the satisfaction with various types of facilities, as well as of the reasons for choosing specific facilities, is difficult to gain with the limited information available in national surveys, this chapter relies more than the previous chapters on the fieldwork carried in April-June 2010 in Ghana and Burkina Faso. It should be emphasized again that the sample size of the fieldwork was limited (see appendix D for a discussion), so that the results in the various tables in this chapter based on the qualitative fieldwork should be considered as indicative only.

The structure of the chapter is the same as in the previous three. Before presenting detailed evidence for Ghana and Burkina Faso, cross-country evidence from household surveys on the satisfaction of users with various types of facilities is presented in section 2. Section 3 then looks at Ghana and Burkina Faso in more depth. A brief conclusion follows.

Cross-Country Evidence

While there are statements about FISs providing better-quality services resulting in more satisfied students or parents, and possibly also in terms of better outcomes (attainment and achievement), much of the evidence for developing countries comes from qualitative work and small-scale surveys. Evidence from national surveys remains thin. This section relies on data from seven of the surveys used previously (see table 7.1) in order to measure rates of satisfaction with the education services provided FISs as compared to other private and public facilities.

The results are provided in tables 7.2 and 7.3 for primary and secondary education. In the case of primary education, with the exception of Burundi, FISs again appear to enjoy higher satisfaction rates than public facilities. For the population as a whole, the satisfaction rate among FISs is almost four to five percentage points above that of public providers in the two focus countries (Burkina Faso and Ghana), while it is higher by more than 10 points in Niger, almost 20 points in Senegal, and about 40 points or even more in Mali and the Republic of Congo. In Burundi, the satisfaction rate with FISs is eight points below that for public facilities. As to the comparison of FISs with other private facilities, FISs appear to have the upper hand in one country (Mali), while other private providers do better in four countries (Burundi, Ghana, Senegal, and the Republic of Congo), with the last country (Niger) being a tie. Satisfaction rates are higher in urban than rural areas, and they also tend to increase with the quintile of well-being of households—this is the case in all countries, except Niger, but for that country satisfaction rates are so high that interpretation is more difficult.

For secondary education, the differences between FISs and public schools tend to be small in the population as a whole for Burkina Faso, Burundi, Ghana, and Niger but in the other three countries, FISs do better than public schools. In three countries (Burundi, Ghana, and Niger) private secular schools tend to have the highest rates of satisfaction. FISs perform best in Burkina Faso, Senegal, the Republic of Congo, and Mali. This suggests that the comparative performance of FISs is stronger at the secondary than at the primary level.

What are the main reasons for nonsatisfaction? Even if there are slight differences between the surveys, the questionnaires typically identify the following potential reasons: lack of books/supplies, poor teaching, lack of teachers, facilities in bad condition, overcrowding, lack of furniture, and other problems. In a few

Table 7.1 Countries in the Sample with Data on Satisfaction in Education Modules

Country (survey name)	Year of implementation	Country (survey name)	Year of implementation
Burundi (QUIBB)	2006	Niger (QUIBB)	2005
Burkina Faso (QUIBB)	2007	Congo, Rep. (QUIBB)	2005
Ghana (CWIQ)	2003	Senegal (ESPS)	2005/06
Mali (QUIBB)	2006		

Source: World Bank data.

Table 7.2 Satisfaction Rates with Primary Education Services
percent

	Residence area		Welfare quintile					Total
	Urban	Rural	Q1	Q2	Q3	Q4	Q5	
Burkina Faso, 2007								
Public	86.0	82.3	76.3	82.0	82.8	83.3	86.9	83.0
Faith-inspired	92.1	79.4	56.8	61.8	87.4	84.6	91.6	84.5
Private secular	91.3	73.8	49.0	87.3	67.9	81.7	93.5	88.6
Total	87.7	82.0	75.3	81.7	82.6	83.3	88.3	83.4
Burundi, 2006								
Public	51.8	34.6	29.6	36.3	35.4	36.5	43.0	35.6
Faith-inspired	75.4	24.2	11.6	29.2	31.8	15.2	49.3	25.3
Private secular	75.7	53.6	78.2	27.7	60.6	63.2	76.5	66.5
Total	55.3	34.5	29.9	35.6	35.5	36.3	45.3	35.9
Ghana, 2003								
Public	80.26	61.37	56.9	67.8	71.1	74.1	73.4	67.7
Faith-inspired	81.66	59.49	61.1	70.1	76.0	76.5	75.3	72.0
Private secular	87.67	73.65	69.7	77.8	82.2	85.4	89.2	83.5
Total	82.99	62.66	57.9	69.3	73.8	77.8	79.6	71.3
Senegal, 2005								
Public	75.2	52.3	57.2	55.4	57.5	65.1	77.2	62.1
Faith-inspired	92.3	68.3	55.8	72.1	77.9	88.0	96.1	84.7
Private secular	91.5	68.4	68.6	79.0	68.2	93.1	93.4	90.1
Total	79.1	53.1	57.2	56.5	58.7	68.9	82.8	65.6
Congo, Rep., 2005								
Public	20.4	12.2	16.0	16.0	17.3	17.8	16.9	16.7
Faith-inspired	62.6	14.9	44.0	35.8	56.3	58.5	52.5	51.8
Private secular	69.7	30.8	78.8	43.1	62.4	64.8	68.2	63.0
Total	37.7	14.2	22.9	20.9	29.9	33.1	44.8	28.7
Niger, 2007								
Public	82.9	88.9	87.3	88.3	91.9	87.2	82.8	87.6
Faith-inspired	99.7	100.0	100.0	100.0	99.6	100.0	100.0	99.9
Private secular	99.3	99.7	100.0	100.0	98.9	99.6	99.6	99.6
Total	88.4	92.1	90.5	91.3	93.9	91.0	89.5	91.2
Mali, 2006								
Public	54.3	37.6	40.0	33.5	35.4	48.1	65.2	45.0
Faith-inspired	94.6	81.2	31.3	100.0	80.1	89.5	95.9	91.1
Private secular	88.8	48.9	30.5	50.5	64.7	76.4	90.6	80.0
Total	62.6	38.5	39.5	34.7	37.4	52.0	73.9	50.4
Average								
Public	64.4	52.8	51.9	54.2	55.9	58.9	63.6	56.8
Faith-inspired	85.5	61.1	51.5	67.0	72.7	73.2	80.1	72.8
Private secular	86.3	64.1	67.8	66.5	72.1	80.6	87.3	81.6
Total	70.5	53.9	53.3	55.7	58.8	63.2	72.0	60.9

Source: Estimates based on national household surveys. See Tsimpo and Wodon 2013b.

Table 7.3 Satisfaction Rates with Secondary Education Services
percent

	Residence area		Welfare quintile					Total
	Urban	Rural	Q1	Q2	Q3	Q4	Q5	
			Burkina Faso, 2007					
Public	82.2	82.5	87.7	89.4	83.2	75.2	84.0	82.3
Faith-inspired	85.0	83.3	100.0	14.6	72.0	75.7	91.3	84.7
Private secular	84.2	48.3	100.0	56.8	54.3	68.4	86.2	81.3
Total	83.2	80.8	89.0	82.4	79.6	74.0	85.4	82.3
			Burundi, 2006					
Public	61.0	36.1	27.3	42.9	35.1	37.6	46.8	39.3
Faith-inspired	85.6	27.3	11.3	69.7	0	51.0	56.9	38.9
Private secular	60.8	55.2	36.5	50.6	58.4	38.1	64.9	59.5
Total	61.9	36.2	25.8	43.8	36.4	37.7	52.0	41.7
			Ghana, 2003					
Public	81.7	74.93	71.7	77.7	80.3	81.1	82.8	79.7
Faith-inspired	83.27	60	48.8	72.9	89.1	72.5	82.0	76.4
Private secular	87.25	67.85	74.1	71.6	86.6	80.7	89.6	82.7
Total	82.47	73.76	70.9	77.0	81.3	80.8	83.8	79.9
			Senegal, 2005					
Public	72.3	56.1	54.2	61.2	63.4	69.3	75.5	67.3
Faith-inspired	90.3	54.3	36.4	70.3	82.1	75.9	95.1	84.2
Private secular	81.9	54.6	57.0	61.6	77.6	79.3	85.7	80.8
Total	75.1	56.0	53.7	61.6	64.9	70.7	79.2	69.9
			Congo, Rep., 2005					
Public	20.0	14.2	22.4	19.0	19.1	18.8	14.6	19.0
Faith-inspired	73.4	—	40.2	79.0	86.4	84.1	78.9	73.4
Private secular	60.9	43.2	71.7	49.4	67.7	55.9	59.7	59.4
Total	30.2	17.6	25.9	24.0	29.5	30.5	31.3	28.3
			Niger, 2007					
Public	80.2	96.9	97.3	89.0	94.7	83.5	82.0	86.8
Faith-inspired	85.4	100.0	—	—	100.0	100.0	75.1	87.6
Private secular	97.8	—	100.0	100.0	100.0	83.7	98.4	97.8
Total	84.8	96.9	97.4	89.5	95.0	83.7	87.3	88.7
			Mali, 2006					
Public	53.4	45.5	56.5	40.0	47.2	46.4	58.1	51.3
Faith-inspired	100.0	77.5	—	—	100.0	47.1	—	83.9
Private secular	84.8	23.6	34.1	72.8	39.8	56.4	91.5	78.5
Total	57.3	44.8	55.7	41.8	47.5	47.2	63.2	54.2
			Average					
Public	64.4	58.0	59.6	59.9	60.4	58.8	63.4	60.8
Faith-inspired	86.1	67.1	47.3	61.3	75.7	72.3	79.9	75.6
Private secular	79.7	48.8	67.6	66.1	69.2	66.1	82.3	77.1
Total	67.9	58.0	59.8	60.0	62.0	60.7	68.9	63.6

Source: Estimates based on national household surveys. See Tsimpo and Wodon 2013b.
Note: — = not available.

countries, cost is also included as a potential reason, but not in most. At the primary level, the lack of books and supplies is the main reason for nonsatisfaction in virtually all countries. Overcrowding and lack of teachers are also often mentioned, as well as many of the other problems. In secondary schools, the lack of books/supplies also comes first in most countries, but the lack of teachers comes up more often as a reason for nonsatisfaction. It should be emphasized that the fact that the cost of schooling is not a major complaint does not mean that it is not an issue. The questions are asked only to parents who have children in school—among parents who have children of school age who are not enrolled, cost is often the main or at least a key reason for not being in school, but this is not shown here since that information cannot be disaggregated according to the type of provider given that the children are not in school.

Additional Evidence for Ghana and Burkina Faso

Reasons for Choosing FISs in Ghana

What are the reasons for choosing faith-inspired schools as they emerge from the qualitative and small sample data on satisfaction with education services in Ghana? As shown in table 7.4 among parents sending their children to Christian schools, faith is a key motivation for half (50.0 percent) of the parents. The share is even higher at 75.0 percent for parents sending their children to Islamic schools (37.5 percent of parents in Islamic schools also mentioned that learning Arabic was a motivation for enrolling their children in the school, probably because Arabic is needed for reading the Qur'an). This importance of religion is observed among almost all of those who choose faith-inspired schools, as a few quotes from the in-depth interviews illustrate: "The school is strict and disciplines the children. Apart from academic subjects, Christian values are instilled

Table 7.4 **Main Reasons for Choosing the School, Qualitative Fieldwork, 2010**
percent

	Parents at Islamic schools	Parents at Christian schools	Parents at secular schools
Location	20.8	16.7	37.5
Religion	75.0	50.0	6.3
Morals, values, behavior	—	29.2	—
To learn Arabic	37.5	—	—
To learn English	4.2	—	—
Teacher quality, discipline	4.2	33.3	25.0
Academic results	4.2	16.7	25.0
Child's future schooling/job	4.2	4.2	—
Familiarity with the school	16.7	16.7	18.8
Low or no fees	4.2	—	31.3
Low cost books and supplies	4.2	—	—
Teaching contents/curriculum	29.2	4.2	—

Source: Ghana fieldwork. See Shojo and Wodon 2013.
Note: Multiple answers allowed. — = not available.

in the children, and that makes them obedient" (Parent at a public Christian school); "Because this school is an Islamic school, they teach Arabic and English. That is why I prefer this school to secular schools" (Parent at a public Islamic school); "Children in the other schools are not as disciplined like the children here. The fear of the Lord is taught and also the church supports us. I want my children to be brought up in the Christian faith" (Parent at a private Christian school).

In addition to the role of faith and values, quality also mattered, especially for parents relying on Christian schools. For some of these parents, quality could lead to changing school. As a parent who withdrew her daughter from a Christian school to send her to a better public Islamic school: "I am Christian. My daughter was in a Christian school before but I removed her and sent her to this school, because teachers are very good and this school produces a lot of children who pass the national examination and go to secondary schools."

Another question was asked about the advantages of the school chosen by parents (table 7.5). Faith and values came again strongly as key advantages among those sending their children to Christian and Islamic schools. Among parents interviewed in secular schools on the other hand, location and the absence of school fees were the most important reasons for the choice of the schools. As a parent sending her children to a secular school explains: "The school is a community school, so it is open for community. I want to keep an eye on the children since it is close to my house. Additionally, I don't have to worry about school fees."

Still another question was asked to parents on what children should learn in school (table 7.6). In secular schools, mathematics and science as well as English came up as important areas of study. These areas are also important for parents sending their children to faith-inspired schools, but less so. Again, parents in

Table 7.5 Advantages of the School You Selected, Qualitative Fieldwork, 2010
percent

	Parents at Islamic schools	Parents at Christian schools	Parents at faith-inspired schools	Parents at secular schools
No or low fees	—	—	—	18.8
Low cost books and supplies	—	—	—	12.5
Free or low cost meals	—	—	—	6.3
Religion	66.7	62.5	64.6	—
Morals, values, behavior, attitudes	50.0	83.3	66.7	—
To learn Arabic	50.0	—	25.0	—
To learn English	20.8	—	10.4	—
Leader quality	—	—	—	6.3
Teacher quality, discipline, seriousness	—	8.3	4.2	—
Test results, advantage for children's future	—	4.2	2.1	—

Source: Ghana fieldwork. See Shojo and Wodon 2013.
Note: Multiple answers allowed. The sum of the answers for secular schools is below 100 percent because many parents did not identify specific comparative advantages. — = not available.

Table 7.6 What Should Children Learn at School? Qualitative Fieldwork, 2010
percent

	Parents at Islamic schools	Parents at Christian schools	Parents at faith-inspired schools	Parents at secular schools
General knowledge	16.7	25.0	20.8	12.5
Religion	4.2	20.8	12.5	12.5
Morals, values, behavior, attitudes	29.2	54.2	41.7	25.0
Literacy (reading and writing)	4.2	4.2	4.2	18.8
Mathematics and science	58.3	58.3	58.3	87.5
Arabic	45.8	0	22.9	0
English	70.8	54.2	62.5	62.5
Life skills (health, hygiene, sexuality)	4.2	4.2	4.2	0
Vocational training (farming, tailoring, computer etc.)	12.5	4.2	8.3	18.8
Other language skills	20.8	8.3	14.6	18.8

Source: Ghana fieldwork. See Shojo and Wodon 2013.
Note: Multiple answers allowed.

faith-inspired schools regard morals, values, behavior, and attitudes as a key area of learning, and much more so than parents in secular schools. As stated by a parent relying on a private Christian school: "When children attend religious schools, there is a difference in their behavior. My children's behavior is different from those who attend public schools." A parent relying on a private Islamic school stated: "When the children complete this type of school, they will be knowledgeable in both academic subjects and Islamic studies." By contrast, at least some parents sending their children to secular schools do not approve of religion's influence in school. One such parent explained that "Education is general. There is no ideology or religious group interference, which could frustrate teachers and children"; another argued that "Some religious schools sometimes force their beliefs and doctrines on children so it is advantageous for me to let my child go to a secular school so that she learns what everybody believes in."

Faith also matters for principals and school owners. It is a key reason for establishing faith-inspired schools. Apart from providing education to local children by the local community, the reasons for setting up faith-inspired schools include raising good Muslims or Christians, and teaching both religious and secular topics. As a private Christian school owner put it: "We did not have any private religious school in the area before. So we decided to set up a religious school. This school was established in 1991. All of the teachers are local. That is good for children." A private Islamic school owner emphasized the importance of religious education: "We lacked schools in this area. The school was established in 2002. Muslim communities around this area were very vulnerable. We decided to give people empowerment and education. We educate Islamic faith, values and practice to be a good Muslim." The same emphasis was noted by a head teacher in another Islamic school: "Parents saw that there was a need to set up Islamic school to educate children about Islam. In 1963, the school was established with support of an Islamic NGO outside the country and then the government absorbed it. Now it is only one public Islamic school in this area… The students learn Arabic in addition to secular subjects."

The emphasis on faith and values in faith-inspired schools does not mean however that the schools do not accept children from all faiths. Interviews with school leaders suggest that indeed all faith-inspired schools accept children who belong to a religion different from that of the school. Still, there were differences in terms of the religion of the children enrolled. At Christian schools, 87.5 percent of the parents interviewed were Christian, which is a bit higher than the share of Christians in the national population, but not extremely so. By contrast among parents interviewed at Islamic schools, 91.7 percent were Muslim. Thus, while many Muslims go to Christian schools, few Christians go to Islamic schools.

Finally, as shown in table 7.7, most parents appear satisfied with the quality of teachers in their schools and academic performance, despite evidence from test scores that suggest low levels of achievements. However, in public schools, 83.4 percent of parents appear to be dissatisfied with the resources available to their schools, and the lack of satisfaction is similar in secular private schools. By contrast, 66.7 percent of parents in faith-inspired schools appear to be satisfied with the resources available in the schools. This result is surprising, but it may be due to the small sample size in the qualitative fieldwork.

In the sample of schools for the qualitative fieldwork, faith-inspired schools that do not receive public funding have a high share of teachers who are not formally certified as per the guidelines of the Ghana Educational Service (GES). In public schools (both faith inspired and secular), teachers are recruited directly by GES and receive in-service teacher training. By contrast, private schools recruit teachers independently, which results in a large share of teachers without certification. This does not mean however that the performance of those teachers is substandard, given the ability of private schools to fire teachers that would not perform adequately. As the head teacher at a private Christian school explained it: "When recruiting teachers, we advertise. Then people apply and we have interviews with them. Their qualification is assessed to know if they can teach children and which classes they can handle. I have worked in public schools for more than 25 years. In this school, I am the only qualified teacher and others are not qualified… Some did not complete secondary school… But we train them on how to make a lesson plan, how to give lessons, how to discipline the children,

Table 7.7 **Evaluation of Schools by Parents, Qualitative Fieldwork, Ghana 2010**
percent

	School resources			Quality of teachers			Academic performance		
	Positive	*Neutral*	*Negative*	*Positive*	*Neutral*	*Negative*	*Positive*	*Neutral*	*Negative*
FISs	66.7	0	33.3	95.8	0	4.2	87.5	12.5	0
Public	16.7	0	83.4	95.7	4.4	0	70.8	12.5	16.7
Private secular	0	12.5	87.5	100.0	0	0	75.0	18.8	6.3

Source: Ghana fieldwork. See Shojo and Wodon 2013.
Note: Positive corresponds to parents declaring being very satisfied or satisfied. Negative corresponds to parents declaring being dissatisfied or very dissatisfied.

everything. We educate them to become a good teacher." While perceptions of teacher quality are as high in private faith-inspired schools as in other schools in the sample, it might still be beneficial to have private school teachers benefitting from in-service training that the GES provides for teachers serving in public schools.

Reasons for Choosing FISs in Burkina Faso

In the Burkina Faso fieldwork, parents also tend to be satisfied with the schools they send their children to, whether one considers teacher quality, academic results, school resources, school goals, student behavior, and specific topics. Christian schools tend to have a higher satisfaction than Islamic schools, followed by public schools. There are some differences, but not necessarily major ones—for example, parents relying on Christian and Islamic schools might be very satisfied with the academics, while parents using public schools might be less satisfied. As regards relationships with the community however, Islamic schools had a higher satisfaction rate than public and Christian schools—this relates to whether the school is concerned with community well-being, whether it supports community projects and activities, and whether it provides assistance for the poorest community members.

In all schools, parents suggested that improvements could be made in some areas. One in five parents in Christian schools mentioned overcrowding and 40 percent suggested the need to improve and expand facilities. Overcrowding was even more of an issue in the public schools with about half of the parents citing this problem. In Islamic schools, 38.7 percent of parents said that the level of the school fees was beyond their means. In addition, 32.3 percent said that the schools lacked resources, 19.1 percent said that facilities needed improvement, and 16.1 percent suggested that the teachers' performance was inadequate.

Some parents complained about uneven academic performance in Franco-Arab schools and thought that quality could be further improved, especially through better trained teachers. Examples of such complaints are as follows: "[The teachers] are not trained… To educate children requires a mastery of certain techniques, a pedagogical knowledge. It would be good for the school to train the teachers to improve their performance"; "There is a problem with the teachers. There are many young teachers who lack experience and qualifications. They are amateurs, young people in search of work"; "Certain pupils are characterized by their good performance but there are many who are not… There is [too much] religious education, which is not subject to evaluation." Yet other parents offered positive comments about what they viewed as a more holistic and well-rounded education: "The students learn both Arabic and French. They also learn to master the Qur'an and pray correctly. They are cultivated and have a sharp and open mind compared to students in the public schools"; "The school manages to achieve its goals by transmitting a quality education and by giving the children an exemplary education based on the Islamic faith…. The teachers perform well because in spite of their meager wages, they are conscientious and stress the education of the children."

Satisfaction and Preferences

Table 7.8 Reasons for Choosing the School over Other Options, Burkina Faso
percent

	Parents at Islamic schools	Parents at Christian schools	Parents at public schools
Location	38.7	33.3	70.0
Religious classes/identity, learning to be Muslim/Christian	83.9	33.3	—
Moral education (values, behavior)	35.5	36.7	—
To learn Arabic	29.0	—	—
To learn French	25.8	—	3.3
School administrator quality (headmaster)	9.7	6.7	3.3
Teacher quality: Knowledgeable, conscientious, effective	12.9	46.7	10.0
Academic results, test results	25.8	76.7	46.7
Child's future (better education, work opportunities)	9.7	6.7	16.7
Familiarity with this school	—	6.7	13.3
No or low school fees	—	—	30.0
Lack of religious proselytizing	—	—	16.7

Source: Burkina Faso fieldwork. See Gemignani and Wodon 2013.
Note: Multiple answers allowed. — = not available.

What about the reasons for choosing faith-inspired schools? The education provided by faith-inspired schools is valued by the individuals and communities that they serve, for reasons related to both quality and the promotion of religious and moral values, but with some differences in the motivations of parents in Franco-Arab (Islamic), Christian, and public schools. As shown in table 7.8, parents at Christian schools said that they chose their school for its academic and teacher quality (76.7 percent and 46.7 percent, respectively). By contrast, respondents in Islamic schools more often said that their choice of school was largely based on the opportunity for their children to receive a religious education (83.9 percent), with smaller numbers listing academic or teacher quality (25.8 percent and 12.9 percent respectively). In public schools, location was a deciding factor for 70 percent of parents, followed by academic quality (46.7 percent) and the lack of school fees (30.0 percent). Education on moral values was listed as a reason for school choice by about a third of parents in Islamic and Christian schools, but by no parents in public schools.

As shown in table 7.9, when asked about the most important area of study for their children, the top response for parents sending their children in Franco-Arab schools is religious education (32.3 percent), followed by moral education and literacy (22.6 percent each). In contrast, a larger share of parents at Christian schools stated literacy (53.3 percent) or knowledge (13.3 percent) as the priority, followed by moral education (13.3 percent) and religious education (3.3 percent). Less than a quarter of parents in Christian schools ranked religion in their top three goals, versus three-quarters in Franco-Arab schools. Parents at secular schools followed the Christian schools pattern (43.3 percent literacy, 16.7 percent knowledge, 26.7 percent moral values, 3.3 percent religion).

Table 7.9 Comparison of Various Schools in Burkina Faso, Burkina Faso
percent

	Parents at Islamic schools	Parents at Christian schools	Parents at public schools
	Most important area of study		
Knowledge—general	3.3	13.3	16.7
Religious education	32.3	3.3	3.3
Moral education	22.6	13.3	26.7
Literacy (reading, writing)	22.6	53.3	43.3
Arabic	6.5	—	—
French	3.3	13.3	3.3
Music, art	—	3.3	3.3
Life skills (health, hygiene, sex education)	—	—	3.3
Vocational training	6.5	—	—
All	100	100	100
	Educational goal of highest importance		
Betterment of society	25.8	3.3	13.3
Moral development	22.6	10.0	3.3
Academic achievement	32.3	86.7	83.3
Spiritual development	19.4	—	—
Total	100	100	100
	Performance of your school as compared to other schools		
Higher standard	38.7	83.3	63.3
Same standard	41.9	16.7	23.3
Lower standard	3.2	—	3.3
Don't know, missing	16.1	—	10.0
Total	100	100	100
	Benefit of the school for the community		
General academic advantages, literacy, etc.	29.0	20.0	43.4
Moral education	41.9	23.3	6.7
Religious education/spiritual guidance	41.9	20.0	—
Religious community and identity	32.3	—	—
Future work/academic opportunities for youth	6.5	16.7	33.3
None/don't know	—	36.7	26.7

Source: Burkina Faso fieldwork. See Gemignani and Wodon 2013.
Note: Multiple answers allowed. — = not available.

Parents were also asked to choose the educational goal of highest importance, among social, moral, academic and spiritual goals. One-fifth of parents in Islamic schools selected spiritual goals (19.4 percent) versus no parents at Christian schools. Furthermore, one quarter of parents at Islamic schools selected the betterment of society as the most important educational goal. This is closely related to a view of education as a means for improving community well-being and self-determination. Indeed, when asked about community benefits from the schools, parents in Islamic schools listed a range of advantages related to the role of religious and moral education in the lives of children and their families. Christian school parents discussed both academic and moral/religious advantages to the community. In secular schools, the role of religious and moral education did not come up in a major way in the answers. As for the students, the vast majority of parents at Christian and secular schools selected academic achievement as the most important goal. Finally, while most parents in Christian schools feel that their school has very high performance standards as compared to the public system, parents at Islamic schools are fairly evenly split between those who state that academic standards are about the same as in the public schools, and those who state that the standards in the Franco-Arab schools are higher.

It is important to note that many parents in all types of schools value moral education, even though it does not always show up at the top of a list of goals or as an important factor in choosing a school. A large percentage of parents at all schools listed moral values as one of their top three educational goals (48.4 percent at Islamic schools, 80 percent at Christian schools, and 70 percent at public schools), and more than half of parents in both Islamic and Christian schools cited moral education as a key advantage of faith-based schools. But Christian schools are attended by children of all faiths, and religious education is not emphasized in the curriculum. Rather, the schools stress moral values in addition to secular subjects. Several school leaders pointed out that the recent agreement between the Catholic leadership and the state (while providing subsidies for teacher salaries) has made it particularly important that the national curriculum be strictly followed, which leaves little time for religious education. The Protestant schools visited had a similar approach. In both types of school, 15 minutes to 2 hours per week may be devoted to religious instruction and this is limited to a short prayer at the beginning and end of the day, songs, and, in some schools, Biblical lessons on morality. In the Catholic schools, children who are not Christian pray or meditate during prayer time, following their own faith practices. More formal instruction (Bible studies, catechism) takes place outside of school hours.

Overall, what emerges from this analysis is fairly similar to the findings for Ghana. Faith matters for the choice of a school, at least for parents sending their children to faith-inspired schools, and this is especially the case for Islamic schools. Christian schools tend to have the highest academic standard, while the situation is more mixed for Islamic schools. The issue of quality in Islamic schools has been identified in previous work, and been related among others to the role of *marabous*, a specific type of Islamic teacher (Hagberg 2002; Yaro 1994), as well as the fact that many parents sending their children to Islamic schools view Qu'ranic education as more important than other topics (De Lange 2007) which may lead some Muslim children to attend nonformal Islamic schools (Kürzinger et al. 2008). This can lead to difficult choices for Muslim parents between sending their children to an Islamic school emphasizing religious studies and a Christian school with higher academic standards. To some extent, the rise mostly in urban areas of new Franco-Arab schools that integrate Islamic education and secular subjects is a response to this dilemma (Hagberg 2002).

Performance of Education Services in Ghana

Satisfaction rates are not a measure of performance, if performance is understood as related to human development outcomes. In the case of education, performance is often measured through test scores, but the available data on test scores, for example on Ghana, do not identify students in faith-inspired schools separately (George and Wodon 2013). An alternative is to rely on subjective perceptions of literacy (reading and writing) and numeracy which are available in the surveys used for this study. These assessments are typically made by the household head. They are substantially less precise than test scores, but nevertheless useful. The assessment provided in this section for Ghana is based on data from the GLSS5, with the objective to compare faith-inspired schools to public and private secular schools (as mentioned in previous chapters both Christians and Islamic schools are considered together—the two categories cannot be disaggregated in the data).

Five questions are asked to each child in the survey aged five years and above: Can the child read in English? Can s/he read a Ghanaian language? Can s/he write in English? Can s/he write in a Ghanaian language? Can s/he do written calculation? The focus in this section is on reading and writing in English, and written calculation (this is because much fewer children read and write in a Ghanaian language than in English). Basic statistics on the answers to these questions for the sample of children aged 10–15 who are attending a primary school at the time of the survey are provided in table 7.10 nationally, as well as by gender, by quintile of well-being, and by urban-rural residence area. In the national sample, 65.0 percent of the students in public schools can read in

Table 7.10 Literacy and Numeracy in Primary School, Children Aged 10–15, Ghana
percent

	Quintiles					Areas		Gender		
	1st	2nd	3rd	4th	5th	Rural	Urban	Female	Male	Total
	Public									
Reading in English	59.0	59.3	66.0	78.7	81.5	59.3	80.1	64.1	65.8	65.0
Writing in English	52.4	54.7	60.5	72.1	77.8	53.6	74.4	58.1	60.6	59.4
Written calculation	86.8	89.4	88.7	95.1	95.4	87.7	94.9	88.8	90.5	89.7
	Religious									
Reading in English	17.2	68.7	72.1	88.4	93.9	50.7	89.6	70.1	72.3	71.3
Writing in English	17.2	58.0	61.6	73.3	89.7	42.4	82.0	66.0	60.8	63.3
Written calculation	79.8	85.6	86.6	100.0	100.0	86.0	97.3	88.2	95.3	91.9
	Private (non religious)									
Reading in English	80.1	79.7	89.6	92.3	96.8	82.6	94.1	90.7	88.2	89.4
Writing in English	75.8	68.6	84.7	89.0	88.8	72.2	90.7	83.1	83.1	83.1
Written calculation	91.4	94.1	95.6	97.9	98.5	94.6	97.3	96.8	95.7	96.2
	All									
Reading in English	58.4	61.7	69.7	82.4	87.5	60.8	84.2	68.0	69.1	68.6
Writing in English	52.2	56.2	64.0	75.8	82.5	54.7	78.9	61.8	63.5	62.7
Written calculation	86.8	89.7	89.6	96.1	96.9	88.2	95.7	89.8	91.4	90.7

Source: Estimates based on GLSS5. See Adoho and Wodon 2013c.

English, and the proportion is 59.4 percent for writing in English. The corresponding shares are higher in faith-inspired schools, at respectively 71.3 percent and 63.3 percent, and even higher in other private schools, at 89.4 percent and 83.1 percent. Similarly, the proportion of students who can do a written calculation is lower in public schools, at 89.7 percent, than in faith-inspired and other private schools, at 91.9 percent and 96.2 percent.

There are differences between quintiles of well-being, as well as between rural and urban areas in subjective measures of literacy and numeracy. In many cases, students in the lower quintiles tend to have a likelihood of being able to read, write, or compute up to 30 percentage points below those in the top quintiles (and in one case—that of students in the bottom quintile attending faith-inspired schools, the difference is even larger, but that sample is small). Note that in urban areas, students in FISs do better than students in public schools, but in rural areas, the reverse is observed, especially for reading and writing. It is likely that the lower subjective measures of literacy in rural areas are related in part to the very low measures of literacy among students in FISs who belong to the bottom quintile of well-being, since most students in that quintile live in rural areas.

Given the selection process that goes on both across and within families as to whom will go to which type of school, simple statistical differences in perceived literacy and numeracy between the three types of schools need not reflect differences in school performance. For example, if within a neighborhood the best students are sent to private schools, which tend to be more expensive, this could explain part of the higher measures of literacy and numeracy observed in those schools. To correct for such bias, regression analysis is needed, taking into account the fact that the selection of school may depend on the performance of the student (instrumentation for the choice of school is required; this is done using the leave-out mean primary sampling unit (PSU) market shares by type of school, as explained in chapter 2, with bootstrapping used in the second stage regressions to correct standard errors).

The independent variables for the various regressions (school choice and subjective indicators of literacy and numeracy) include (1) the type of school attended by the child; (2) the geographic location of the child according to urban or rural status and the main regions in the country; (3) the quintile of consumption per equivalent adult of the household in which the child lives; (4) the religion of the child (with Catholic being the reference category); (5) the sex of the child, whether this is the elder child, and whether the father and mother live in the household; (6) some information on time use for the child that is less likely to be endogenous, and who pays for schooling in the household; (7) the grade in which the child is with the first grade of primary school being the reference category; and (8) information about the level of schooling of the household head and the spouse of the head when there is one.

The full set of regressions is available in Adoho and Wodon (2013c). The school choice regressions suggest that the religion of the child is not a key determinant of school choice, with two exceptions: other Christian children (those who are neither Catholic nor Protestant) and children whose parents declare not having a religion are less likely to go to faith-inspired schools. Another key result is that children from wealthier households are less likely to enroll in faith-inspired schools, although the effect is not systematic. A higher education level for the household head and spouse makes it more likely that the child will go to a faith-inspired school, whereas a child in a female-headed household has a higher probability of going to a public school. Employment type for the household head or spouse does not have much impact on school choice, but the leave-out participation rate in faith-inspired schools is highly statistically significant, and the impact is large as expected.

The key results for the type of schools attended and how this affects literacy and numeracy are provided in table 7.11 (the full set of regressions is provided in appendix G). As compared to public schools, and controlling for other characteristics, attending a faith-inspired school does not have a statistically significant effect on the likelihood of being able to read in English, but it reduces the probability of writing in English. These effects are for rural areas, and thus confirm the message from the basic statistics in table 7.9. For urban areas, in addition to those effects, one must take into account the interaction effects between the faith-inspired school and the urban dummy variables. Only the interaction effect for reading is positive and statistically significant, but the combined effect of the religious dummy and the urban interaction effect would not be statistically significant. Students in private secular schools, on the other hand, do perform better than those in public schools.

A number of other results not shown in table 7.11 are worth noting. The performance of children is better in the Greater Accra region than in other regions, and in urban versus rural areas, but the quintile of well-being of the household to which a student belongs often do not have a statistically significant impact controlling for other variables, except for the top quintile, nor does the faith affiliation of the child in most cases. Boys tend to do better than girls, while other child characteristics and whether the father or mother is living in the household do not matter much. Children who spend more time on housekeeping actually do better in terms of all three subjective indicators of learning. If a child is in a higher grade, the likelihood of being able to read, write, or compute is much higher, as one would expect. A higher education for the household head

Table 7.11 Selected Correlates of Subjective Literacy and Numeracy, Ghana

	Reading in English	Writing in English	Written calculation
Schools/areas (reference: public/rural)			
Religious	−0.294	−0.082*	0.007
Private	0.205*	0.186**	0.037
Religious and urban	0.124*	0.109	0.034
Private and urban	0.105***	−0.108*	−0.003
Urban	0.099***	0.133***	0.023*

Source: Adoho and Wodon 2013c.
Note: Statistical significance levels: *=10 percent, **=5 percent, ***=1 percent.

is sometimes associated with higher performance for the child, but this is far from systematic for the household head, while it matters more for the spouse of the head. Who pays for the education of the child within the household (the head or the spouse) does not seem to make a difference.

Conclusion

This chapter was devoted to an assessment of the satisfaction of users with the quality of services provided by various types of schools, and to the reasons for selecting a specific school. Both national surveys and results from the qualitative fieldwork implemented in Ghana and Burkina Faso were used. Two main findings emerge from the analysis of both types of data.

First, cross-country data suggest that FISs have better satisfaction rates among their clientele than public facilities, but lower satisfaction rates than private secular facilities. The fact that despite limited resources FISs seem to better serve their users than public facilities is encouraging for the work that these institutions do. The appreciation for this work by users also appeared clearly in the qualitative fieldwork for Ghana and Burkina Faso. As to the higher satisfaction rate still for private secular facilities, it is not too surprising, given that these facilities tend to be more expensive and thereby can afford to provide better services. Also, the emphasis on religious education placed in FISs, and especially in Islamic schools, as well as the focus on values in Christian schools, are appreciated by parents, and this is a key reason for some parents to choose to send their children to those schools.

Second, high satisfaction rates need not translate into higher measures of performance in terms of education outcomes. In the case analyzed here on subjective perceptions of literacy and numeracy in Ghana, there are essentially no statistically significant differences in outcomes between faith-inspired and public schools (both Christians and Islamic—the two categories could not be disaggregated), while there is evidence that private secular schools do better. Qualitative evidence suggests that Christian schools that focus more on academics may have better performing students, but this may not apply to Islamic schools, although there is heterogeneity between Franco-Arab urban schools that may do well and small rural Islamic schools reaching the poor, but where opportunities are more limited. Possibly some of these schools that have a strong focus on religious education may invest less in other subjects, so that without state funding, the overall quality of the education received by children in these schools may be lower. Better-trained teachers could be one of the ways to improve the education according to the parent's perceptions.

CHAPTER 8

Conclusion

Despite the important role of faith-inspired schools in education service delivery in Africa, remarkably little systematic evidence is available today on their market share, reach to the poor, cost, and satisfaction among users, in comparison with public and private secular facilities. The primary purpose of this study was to build a stronger evidence base on those questions for Sub-Saharan Africa, with more detailed work for Ghana and Burkina Faso.

The first significant finding was that data from household surveys suggest an average market share for faith-inspired schools (FISs) of about 10–15 percent, which is smaller than is often claimed. The second finding was that FISs do typically not reach the poor in absolute terms more than other household groups. This is not surprising, given the barrier for affordability that the school and other fees charged by FISs represent. But in addition, on average FISs also do not reach the poor more than public facilities, even if they do so more than private secular facilities, and may make special efforts to reaching the poor as well as other vulnerable groups within the constraints they face. The third finding was that the cost for households of the services provided by FISs is higher than that of public facilities, possibly because of a lack of access to public funding which then necessitates higher levels of cost recovery, but lower than that of private secular schools. The fourth finding was that FISs have higher satisfaction rates than public facilities, but slightly lower satisfaction rates than private secular facilities. The fifth finding was that parents using FISs place a strong emphasis on religious education and values. This is the case for both Christian and Islamic schools, but especially in Islamic schools in terms of the role played by religious education. The sixth finding was that students in faith-inspired and private schools may perform better than those in public schools, but this may be due in part to self-selection, and more research is needed in this area, especially for FISs, given the potential heterogeneity between FISs in the quality of the services provided.

While the analysis has been conducted for the most part using data from national surveys from 16 countries, other surveys could be used in the future to expand the country coverage of this work. Some of the Multiple Indicators Cluster Surveys (MICSs) recently implemented in Africa have the required information—as an example, the MICS 2010 in Togo identifies the education service provider (public, private secular, private faith-inspired and community school) and it also provides information on education expenditures. More generally, as more data become available, more counties could be added to the analysis. In terms of the scope of the analysis, the data could also be used for assessing other education outcomes, including whether different types of providers are more efficient than others. This could in principle be measured by looking at indicators such as age for grade, repetition, dropouts, and completion rates. In countries where administrative data are available, comparisons of the allocations of resources (for example teachers) could also be made between different types of providers. More work is also needed on differences in performance (for example using test score data) between providers. Finally, the analysis of the private cost of schooling combined with administrative data on public funding for various types of providers could be used to better understand the cost of achieving desirable education outcomes and to generate national education accounts, as has been done in health.

What about policy? This study was devoted to a basic diagnostic of the role of FISs in service provision in education in Sub-Saharan Africa, with additional work for Ghana and Burkina Faso. Policy questions related to the integration of FISs in national education systems have not been discussed much, but work could be done in this area as well given that such integration is likely to present trade-offs for FISs, as well as for donors and line Ministries. This is thus one priority area where further research should be undertaken. At least three points or research items on the agenda are worth emphasising here.

A first important item on the agenda is to conduct more research on how to deal with the risk of duplication of efforts and the lack of harmonization between the programs and interventions of various types of service providers. To minimize these risks, it is important to improve data collection in order to provide detailed pictures of the service delivery landscape at both the local and national levels. But it is also important to promote collaborations—for example though memorandums of understanding between FISs and governments. Mappings of existing interventions and collaborative agreements should ideally also factor in nonfacilities-based services where the role of faith communities may well be important. This is important for government ministries as well as education providers, but also for donors. Within the World Bank for example, this report has relevance for the work-on-service delivery indicators and public-private partnerships carried out by the human development network and the regions.

A second important item on the agenda is to better understand the constraints in which FISs operate, the challenges they face, and the opportunities they offer. Some challenges faced by FISs may also be faced by other types of providers, but others may be specific to FISs. How can FISs maintain in their programs a preferential option for the poor when the sources of revenues available to them are limited and in some cases reduced? How can FISs maintain their distinctive vision and culture while being progressively more integrated into national education systems? How can the capacity of FISs to evaluate their own interventions,

Education in Sub-Saharan Africa • http://dx.doi.org/10.1596/978-0-8213-9965-1

as well as to assess the extent to which they reach the poor, be expanded? FISs do appear to have some comparative advantages, and a better understanding of how exactly they are able to provide services of quality (as measured through satisfaction rates) would be welcome, as would be an analysis of whether specific practices and characteristics of FISs are transferrable to the public sector as well as private secular facilities. Also, how can a voice be given to FISs in policy discussions at the local, national, and international levels for them to share their experience?

Finally, a third sets of questions, not discussed in this study, relates to the impact of faith on behaviors, not only as it relates to the choice of service provider, but also more generally. In many areas such as child marriage, which has implications for education outcomes, faith-related practices and cultural traditions play an important role, underscoring the potential of engaging religious and traditional leaders as well as FISs in efforts to eradicate such practices, or at least their worst aspects. Given that the market share of FISs is smaller than many had thought, and that their reach to the poor is also limited even if their contribution should not be understated, it could very well be that the more important role that faith plays in education is related to the impact of faith on a wide range of behaviors, as opposed to service delivery. Questions related to faith and behaviors that affect education and other human development outcomes are often more difficult to understand, and also more difficult to influence through government policies than issues related directly to service delivery, but certainly not less important to consider.

APPENDIX A

Faith and Formal Models of School Choice: An Illustration

A fundamental tenet of economic analysis, as well as rational choice theory in religious studies, is that service providers, as well as individuals and households, make rational decisions with regards to the practice of their faith. This includes decisions related to the supply and demand for services, which take into account a variety of factors. One such factor is a person's faith—whether on the demand or supply side of service delivery. But other factors such as cost, quality, and location also matter. There is a large literature in economics on modeling decisions by both firms and consumers which is relevant for a discussion of service delivery by different types of providers. It is not possible here to review this literature, but it is useful to give just one simple example of what this literature entails—even if this is a bit technical—in order to illustrate the considerations at work in theoretical and empirical work on those issues.

The example provided here relates to the role of religiosity in private school choice, and the model was provided by Cohen-Zada and Sander (2008). This section simply restates the model, albeit with slightly different symbols and wording to fit the context of this study (Cohen-Zada and Sander consider Catholics and Protestants in the United States; here the discussion is outlined in terms of Muslims and Christians as the focus is on Africa). Each household has one child, and the question is whether the child should be sent to a public, faith-inspired (Christian or Islamic), or private secular school. The utility or welfare of household i, which has a level of religiosity z_i, depends on its consumption of a numeraire good c (this good represents all other goods consumed apart from the education of the child), as well as the academic quality in secular subjects of the school attended by the child, x, and the religious orientation of the school. Cohen-Zada and Sander stipulate the following utility function:

$$U(c_i, x_i, z_i) = \begin{cases} a \ln(c_i) + (1-\alpha)\ln(x_i) + R_S^J + \beta_S^J \cdot z_i + \epsilon_S^J & \text{in faith-inspired school} \\ a \ln(c_i) + (1-\alpha)\ln(x_i) + \epsilon_S^J & \text{in secular school} \end{cases}$$

where R_S^J represents the utility or disutility that a household of faith affiliation J (Christian or Muslim) with no or a low level of religiosity ($z_i = 0$) derives from the religious environment in a faith-inspired school of type S. Even for households with no or low levels of religiosity, the utility of the household is assumed to be higher if the child attends a school of its own faith affiliation, as opposed to a school from a different (or no) faith affiliation.

In the above equation, the matrix $\{\beta_S^J\}$ captures the effect of religiosity on the utility of the household in each type of faith-inspired school. It is assumed first that the household derives a higher utility if it is more religious and the child attends a school of the same affiliation as that of the household. It is also assumed that for any level of religiosity, more utility is derived from sending one's child to a school of one's own faith affiliation. No assumptions are made as to whether a positive or negative utility is derived from sending one's child to a school from a different faith affiliation. The authors further assume that public education is provided free of charge at a uniform level of quality $\bar{x}$. Private schools, whether faith-inspired or not, charge parents for the education provided to their children.

The next assumption is that the price of a specific faith-inspired school for households will be lower in areas where a higher share of the population is of the school's faith affiliation. This could be because other sources of revenues are available to faith-inspired schools in such areas apart from the direct cost-recovery for the schooling services provided (donations may be available), or simply because some of the costs associated with the faith-inspired school can be shared with the local Church or mosque. Still another explanation for differences in prices might be that in areas with a high population density of a specific faith, more schools of that faith affiliation will be available to serve the population, which may reduce transportation costs for parents. Denoting the share of the population that is Catholic by r, so that the share of the population that is Muslim is $1-r$, the price of Christian schools is assumed to be of the following functional form:

$pc = r^{-r_1}$, while the price of Islamic schools is of the form $p_M = (1-r)^{-r_2}$.

By contrast, the price of secular private schools is constant, so that $p_s = p$.

On the basis of those assumptions, and denoting household income by y_i, the authors show that in a simple stochastic framework, the ratio of the probabilities to choose a faith-inspired school (Catholic, π_C, or Islamic, π_M) versus a public school (π_G) will be such that:

$$\log\left(\frac{\pi_C}{\pi_G}\right)^J = f(\alpha) + (1-\alpha)\ln(y_i) + R_C^J + \beta_C^J \cdot z_i + \gamma_1(1-\alpha) \cdot \ln(r) - (1-\alpha) \cdot \ln\bar{x}$$

$$\log\left(\frac{\pi_M}{\pi_G}\right)^J = f(\alpha) + (1-\alpha)\ln(y_i) + R_M^J + \beta_M^J \cdot z_i + \gamma_2(1-\alpha) \cdot \ln(1-r) - (1-\alpha) \cdot \ln\bar{x}$$

These are but some of the relationships derived by the authors from their model. A similar equation can be obtained for the probability of sending one's child to a private secular school versus a public or government school, and comparisons between those schools and faith-inspired schools, as well as between different types of faith-inspired schools can also be made. These relationships formalize in a simple way a few basic assumptions that can then be tested, such as the hypothesis that all other things being equal, households with higher incomes will be more likely to send their children to faith-inspired schools (since public schools are free, and only higher-income households can afford to pay for tuition at a low cost to them in terms of foregone utility), or the hypothesis that the share of the population of a specific faith affiliation in a given area will tend to lead to a higher probability of households of that affiliation sending their children to faith-inspired schools in that area (since this lowers the cost of the schools), and that religiosity affects positively the likelihood to send one's children to faith-inspired schools of one's own faith affiliation (since this enters directly in the utility function of the household). Also, a higher level of quality for public schools will reduce the probability of attending both secular and faith-inspired schools (whether Christian or Muslim) as compared to public schools.

The main point made by Cohen-Zada and Sander in their paper is that failing to control for religiosity induces a bias in the estimation of the determinants of school choice, as well as in the relationship between the type of school attended and some measures of performance. Their various models are estimated using data from the General Social Survey implemented in the United States. The results suggest, as expected, that both faith affiliation and the level of religiosity of households affect the demand for faith-inspired and secular private schools, and that the positive influence of Catholic schooling on student performance (as proxied for example through graduation) may be overestimated when religiosity is not taken into account.

More detailed results for the United States were obtained by Cohen-Zada and Sander in their estimation. For example, they find that for Catholics and fundamentalist Protestants, higher religiosity increases the demand for, respectively, Catholic and fundamentalist Protestant schools, but not for other types of faith-inspired schools. By contrast, for nonfundamentalist Protestants, higher religiosity is associated with a higher demand for nonsectarian private schools, but not for other private (faith-inspired) schools. As to households with no religious affiliation, they are more likely to opt for nonsectarian schools. The authors stress that to some extent, the limited substitutability of the various schools because of differences in faith affiliation may reduce the competitive pressure on schools, with some implications for policies related to vouchers for example. The authors also note that to the extent that households chose their location in function of the availability of different types of school, religiosity may lead to neighborhoods that are more concentrated from a religious point of view, but less so from a pure income point of view, as standard economic models suggest based on competition between states or localities to attract wealthier households.

The type of work done in the present study is in many cases more basic and less technical than what is being done in studies such as that of Cohen-Zada and Sander using richer data sets available for the United States. Yet the present study does also suggest that faith affiliation and implicitly religiosity do matter for school choice, as discussed for example in chapter 7 devoted to the satisfaction with service providers and the reason for choosing faith-inspired providers in Sub-Saharan Africa, and especially in Ghana and Burkina Faso. Unfortunately for the quantitative analysis provided in this study, the multipurpose household surveys used to identify the various types of service providers in education do not include variables that could be used as proxies to measure a household's level of religiosity. This information is also not available in Demographic and Health Surveys. Still the model and analysis of Cohen-Zada and Sander were briefly summarized here because their study shows well and in a simple way how it is feasible to derive testable hypotheses about religious practice—in this case as it relates to the choice of school provider for one's children, within a rational choice theory framework that takes into account not only faith affiliation and religiosity, but also other parameters affecting school choices such as the cost of various schools and their quality.

APPENDIX B

Rationale for Combining Quantitative and Qualitative Data[1]

This study relies on both nationally representative household surveys and qualitative fieldwork data. The combination of quantitative and qualitative data is important and warranted by the nature of some of the questions being analyzed. Quantitative data and methods have long been privileged in the development literature, and especially in economics. They provide robustness to the results if they rely on appropriate samples, and regression analysis helps to control for a large number of other variables when measuring the impact of a specific variable on a given outcome. Yet quantitative data often cannot fully capture causality, especially when the analysis fails to provide appropriate contextual information. Qualitative methods such as participant observation or community surveys with key informant interviews help to shed light on the religious, economic, sociocultural, and political context of the processes under study.

While quantitative analysis in development work is often goods- and services centered, qualitative research is often people centered (for example following Sen's work on the importance of freedom and capabilities to achieve functionings) and institutions centered (since the access to and use of services is driven by processes rather than a condition at a given point of time, the role of institutions in permitting or preventing access must be analyzed). Qualitative research also often contains both objective and subjective dimensions, to the degree that it considers both the objective conditions of people's lives and access to services, and their perceptions about those services, and more generally their feelings about their situation (this can also be done with quantitative data).

An important aspect of qualitative research methods refers to what scholars call research access. While no hasty conclusions should be made about the advantages of qualitative research techniques (respondents may refuse to be interviewed while they may accept to fill in an anonymous questionnaire), such methods are often better suited to address sensitive issues, some of which may be related to faith. In some cases developing a relationship of trust with the "researched" is needed for data collection. The need to adapt the language according to the type of actors under study is also important for the discovery of knowledge (Buchanan, Boddy, and McCalman 1988). In addition, accessing certain types of interviewees such as officials may be hard by simply sending out a questionnaire.

Another argument in favor of integrated research methods relates to the potential of complementing quantitative data with actor-oriented perspectives in applied research. An actor-oriented perspective entails the variety of social practices and often incompatible worldviews between various actors and the multiple realities to which these practices and worldviews respond (Long and Long 1992). In the case of research on service delivery, key actors would include not only the various clients of the organizations providing the services but also the professionals providing those services, whether they work in private or public institutions. The experience and voice of clients, as well as the perspective of government professionals and private facilities' staffs at the different echelons of the service delivery process, are often overlooked when relying only on quantitative survey data, or at least not systematically and rigorously researched.

Still another argument in favor of integrated research methods relates to policy making. Qualitative data derived from interviews and focus groups are often criticized for its subjectivity. This is a legitimate concern, and it underscores the fact that qualitative research methods must be implemented rigorously by well-trained researchers, with their results ideally supported by further quantitative analysis. But policy-oriented social analysis is concerned with change and agency—that is, how the beneficiaries of education services, the staffs in the field manning the facilities, and the policy makers can act outside and sometimes against a system which may reduce access to the services for the poor. In such contexts, the subjectivity of the various actors, and how as persons they perceive their situations of deprivation and/or lack of access to existing services, is crucial to understanding the basis of agency.

A potential problem with formal, objective, and often quantitative methods is that they may take for granted the context and relationships that constitutes the phenomena under study. At the other extreme, a subjective point of view may assert that social reality is an ongoing process that social actors continually reconstruct, failing to see the existing regularities. A key challenge for policy analysis is to analyze the objective conditions of reality while identifying how perceptions influence reality. Especially when it takes into consideration the rules, values, and perceptions of the individuals or groups involved, qualitative research may help to ensure that policies and programs are responsive to the needs of intended beneficiaries in all their social and cultural diversity—including with respect to their faith. And while qualitative methods can help to enrich areas which have traditionally been dominated by quantitative research, the reverse is also true: quantitative methods can enrich these areas which have been dominated by qualitative research. Indeed, the absence or difficulty of quantification has been a factor in the still relatively slow systematic take up of research aiming to measure the contribution of faith-inspired providers of education services in Sub-Saharan Africa.

Note

1. This section follows closely Clert, Gacitua-Mario, and Wodon (2001). On the arguments for combining quantitative and qualitative research methods, see for example Bourdieu and Wacquant (1992), Neuman (1999), and Bamberger (2000).

APPENDIX C

Identification of Faith-Inspired Schools in Multipurpose National Household Surveys

The analysis in this study is based in part on nationally representative multipurpose household surveys with education modules in which the questions on the types of provider used by households for education enables the identification of faith-inspired providers separately from other (secular) private providers. In this appendix, more details are provided on these surveys, and especially on how the questions are asked about the service providers in the questionnaires.

Table C.1 provides the list of the surveys used, together with their exact name and sample size. Table C.2 provides the information on the way in which questions are asked on the types of education providers in the various surveys. All of the modalities that can be chosen by the respondent are assigned to one of three categories: public facilities, faith-inspired facilities, and private secular facilities. Often different surveys ask these questions in different ways, which may be necessary in order to take into account the peculiarities of each country's education system. Note that in most countries only one question is asked about the type of facility used, with the question combining the type of facility used and the type of provider (say public versus private religious). In other countries, two questions are asked, that is households are asked first about the type of facility they use and next whether the facility is public, private-religious, or private non-religious, or some version of this.

Two comments are important to make. First, in many cases, nongovernmental organizations (NGOs) have been included together with faith-inspired providers. This is because in several countries, NGOs are lumped together with faith-inspired schools (FISs) in the way questions are asked in the surveys. To keep the data consistent, where NGOs are identified separately, they have then also been considered as FISs. However, typically the market share of NGOs is much smaller than that of FISs in surveys where the two types of organizations can be assessed separately, so this does not lead to any major bias in the results. In addition, at least some NGOs tend to be faith inspired.

Table C.1 Multipurpose Household Surveys Used for Cross-Country Comparisons

Country	Year	Survey name	Number of households
Burkina Faso	2007	Enquête Annuelle sur les conditions de vie des ménages (EACVM-QUIBB)	8,496
Burundi	2006	Enquête Questionnaire des Indicateurs de Base du Bien être (QUIBB)	7,046
Cameroon	2007	Enquête sur les Conditions des Ménages Camerounais II (ECAM)	11,391
Chad	2003/04	Deuxième Enquête sur la Consommation et le Secteur Informel au Tchad (ECOSIT)	6,697
Congo, Dem. Rep.	2004/05	Enquête 1-2-3 (123 survey)	12,098
Ghana	2003	Core Welfare Indicators Questionnaire Survey (CWIQ)	49,003
Ghana	2005/06	Ghana Living Standards Survey, Fifth round (GLSS)	8,687
Kenya	2005	Kenya Integrated Household Budget Survey (KIHBS)	13,158
Malawi	2004	Malawi Integrated Household Survey (HIS)	11,280
Mali	2006	Enquête Légère. Intégrée auprès des Ménages (ELIM)	4,494
Niger	2007	Enquête nationale sur le budget et la consommation des ménages (ENBC)	4,000
Nigeria	2003/04	Nigeria Living Standards Survey (LMS)	19,158
Congo Rep.	2005	Enquête Congolaise auprès des Ménages pour l'évaluation de la pauvreté (ECOM)	5,002
Senegal	2005	Enquête de Suivi de la Pauvreté au Sénégal (ESPS)	13,568
Sierra Leone	2003	Sierra Leone Integrated Household Survey (SLIHS)	3,720
Swaziland	2009	Swaziland Household Income and Expenditure Survey (SHIES)	3,167
Uganda	2010	Uganda National Household Survey (UNHS)	6,775
Zambia	2004	Zambia Living Conditions Monitoring Survey (LCMS)	19,315

Source: World Bank data. See Tsimpo and Wodon 2013b.

Second, because of the way questions are asked in the surveys, the identification of FISs in some countries may be better than in others, and it is difficult to make a precise country-level assessment of the quality of the identification. At the same time, the cross-check with the UIS data on private sector provision suggests that the data obtained from the surveys reflect relatively well the administrative data.

Table C.2 Identification of the Various Types of Education Facilities

	Public	Faith-inspired	Private secular
Burkina Faso	Public	Private Catholic school, Private Protestant school, Franco-Arab school	Private nonreligious
Burundi	Government, community	Church	Private, other
Cameroon	Public, community school	Mission (day), mission (evening)	Lay private (day), lay private (evening), courses by correspondence or Internet
Congo, Dem. Rep.	Public without convention	Public with convention	Private
Ghana, 2003	Government, community	Religious Organization/Church	Other private, other (specify)
Ghana, 2005/06	Public	Private religious	Private nonreligious
Kenya	Government, community	Private church, private Muslim	Private other, other
Malawi—primary	Lea/government	Church/mission school, Islamic school	Private nonreligious, other primary
Malawi—secondary	Government (conventional), Community day (cdss)	Church/mission school, Islamic school	Night school, other secondary
Mali	Government, community	Religious organization	Private, Other
Niger	Government, community	Religious organization	Private, Other
Nigeria	Federal government, State government, local government	Religious body	Industrial, Private, Other
Congo, Rep.	Government, community	Church	Private, Other
Senegal	French public, community	Franco-Arab school, private Catholic school	Private secular, Other
Sierra Leone	Government, local government	Mission/religious body, Nongovt. organization	Private, Other (specify)
Swaziland	Government	Mission	Private
Uganda	Government	NGO/religious organization	Private, Other
Zambia	Central government, local government	Mission/religious	Industrial, Private, Other (specify)

Source: World Bank data. See Tsimpo and Wodon 2013b.

APPENDIX D

Sample Size for the Qualitative Fieldwork

Part of this study is based on data collected through qualitative fieldwork conducted by the World Bank in Ghana and Burkina Faso between April and June 2010. This appendix provides more details on the procedures that were followed to collect the data, and the sample size in terms of number of facilities, households interviewed, and focus groups.

The fieldwork was designed to answer two questions: (1) how does faith influence the choices of education providers, with a focus on primary schooling and (2) how do different religious communities view the role of religion in their daily lives; for example how does faith shape social norms and decision making regarding marriage and gender relations, health, family planning, inheritance, and labor force participation. The material discussed in this study relates to the first of these two questions.

In the case of education, the data were collected through interviews with parents, head teachers, and school principals for a total of eight or nine schools per country in one urban and one rural location in each of the two countries. The schools were selected with inputs from district education officials, but the main criteria was the requirement that there should be both public and faith-inspired schools in the areas where the qualitative work was conducted—this enabled individuals to discuss the advantages and disadvantages of different types of schools, and to explain the reasons why they chose specific schools. Importantly, the selected areas had to have both Christian and Islamic schools apart from public schools.

The selection of the areas was done in such a way as to have at least two areas—one urban and one rural area—for each of the two countries. In Ghana, faith-inspired schools—whether Christian or Islamic—were categorized in two groups: public and private faith-inspired schools. Public faith-inspired schools are government owned and funded. By contrast, private faith-inspired schools were established by FISs and remain to-date for the most part without government support as well as autonomous even if the curriculum at both the primary and secondary levels follows standards set by the Ghana Education Service.

A semi-structured questionnaire was used to interview households sending their children to the various schools. Each interview took from one hour to one hour and a half, and focused in large part on the perceptions of the schools facilities, as well as the reasons that led individuals to choose one school versus another. Both responses to open-ended questions and to closed questions were obtained. While statistics are derived from the answers to closed questions, they should be considered as indicative only and should not be considered as necessarily representative of the opinions of all of the parents sending their children to various types of schools. This is because respondents were not selected in a purely random way among those using the services from a given facility, and because in addition the sample is small. A separate semi-structured questionnaire was also administered to the school principals and administrators as well as to a few teachers. Finally, a few interviews were conducted with key informants such as officials from government ministries. Summary information on the sample size for data collection is provided in table D.1.

Table D.1 Sample Size for Qualitative Data Collection in Ghana and Burkina Faso

	Ghana	Burkina Faso
Sites/communities		
Number of sites	2	3
Number of facilities	8 (2 Public, 1 Public-Christian, 2 Private-Christian, 2 Public-Islamic, and 1 Islamic schools)	9 (3 Public, 3 Christian, and 3 Islamic schools)
Interviews		
Households/users	64 (8 per school)	90 (10 per school)
Other interviews	Selected interviews of owners/administrators of the education facilities, doctors and teachers, other staffs, religious leaders, and government officials	Selected interviews of owners/administrators of the education facilities, doctors and teachers, other staffs, religious leaders, and government officials
Focus groups		
Sites/communities	2	2
Participants/groups	8–12	8–12
Split by gender/roles	3 (Men, women, and religious leaders)	3 (Men, women, and religious leaders)
Split by religion	3 (Muslims, Christians, and traditional religious groups)	4 (Muslims, Catholics, Protestants, and traditional religious groups)
Number of groups	$18 = 2 \times 3 \times 3$	$24 = 2 \times 3 \times 4$

Source: World Bank data.

APPENDIX E

Standard Errors for Statistical Tables

Many statistical tables with mean values are provided in this study, and they are often large. In order to simplify these tables, standard errors have not been provided, which restricts the ability of the reader to test for statistical significance, or differences between mean values. However, because most of the variables take only values of one or zero, a simple formula can be used to compute the standard errors of the means, if one is willing to assume equal weights for all observations as well as a simple random sample. Denoting the sample size by N, and individual values by x_i, the estimated mean is

$\bar{x} = \frac{1}{N} \Sigma_i^N = 1 x_i$ and the estimated variance is $\hat{V}(\bar{x}) = \frac{1}{N(N-1)} \Sigma_{i=1}^N (x_i - \bar{x})^2$.

If x_i takes only values of zero or one, the variance simplifies into

$$\hat{\sigma}^2(\bar{x}) = \frac{1}{N-1}(\bar{x} - \bar{x}^2)$$

with $\bar{x} = M / N$ where M is number of observations with a value of one. The standard error is simply the squared root value of the variance, so that a typical 95 percent interval of confidence can be computed as:

$$\text{Confidence interval} = \left[\bar{x} - 2\sqrt{\frac{1}{N-1}(\bar{x} - \bar{x}^2)},\ \bar{x} + 2\sqrt{\frac{1}{N-1}(\bar{x} - \bar{x}^2)} \right].$$

The mean value $\bar{x}$ is what is typically presented in the tables, say in terms of the market share of faith-inspired schools (FISs), their reach to the poor, or the satisfaction of users with the services provided by FISs. The formula is a bit more complex if observations have different sampling weights, or if the sample is not a simple random sample but includes for example strata. In those cases the sample size and mean value is not sufficient to compute the exact standard error, but in most cases the confidence interval above would still be a good approximation. Table E.1 provides values of the standard errors for different sample sizes and mean values.

Table E.1 Standard Errors for Means of Dichotomized Variables Under Equal Weights and Simple Random Sampling

Mean value	Sample size							
	20	40	60	100	500	1,000	5,000	10,000
0.05	0.0500	0.0349	0.0284	0.0219	0.0098	0.0069	0.0031	0.0022
0.1	0.0688	0.0480	0.0391	0.0302	0.0134	0.0095	0.0042	0.0030
0.15	0.0819	0.0572	0.0465	0.0359	0.0160	0.0113	0.0051	0.0036
0.2	0.0918	0.0641	0.0521	0.0402	0.0179	0.0127	0.0057	0.0040
0.25	0.0993	0.0693	0.0564	0.0435	0.0194	0.0137	0.0061	0.0043
0.3	0.1051	0.0734	0.0597	0.0461	0.0205	0.0145	0.0065	0.0046
0.35	0.1094	0.0764	0.0621	0.0479	0.0214	0.0151	0.0067	0.0048
0.4	0.1124	0.0784	0.0638	0.0492	0.0219	0.0155	0.0069	0.0049
0.45	0.1141	0.0797	0.0648	0.0500	0.0223	0.0157	0.0070	0.0050
0.5	0.1147	0.0801	0.0651	0.0503	0.0224	0.0158	0.0071	0.0050
0.55	0.1141	0.0797	0.0648	0.0500	0.0223	0.0157	0.0070	0.0050
0.6	0.1124	0.0784	0.0638	0.0492	0.0219	0.0155	0.0069	0.0049
0.65	0.1094	0.0764	0.0621	0.0479	0.0214	0.0151	0.0067	0.0048
0.7	0.1051	0.0734	0.0597	0.0461	0.0205	0.0145	0.0065	0.0046
0.75	0.0993	0.0693	0.0564	0.0435	0.0194	0.0137	0.0061	0.0043
0.8	0.0918	0.0641	0.0521	0.0402	0.0179	0.0127	0.0057	0.0040
0.85	0.0819	0.0572	0.0465	0.0359	0.0160	0.0113	0.0051	0.0036
0.9	0.0688	0.0480	0.0391	0.0302	0.0134	0.0095	0.0042	0.0030
0.95	0.0500	0.0349	0.0284	0.0219	0.0098	0.0069	0.0031	0.0022

APPENDIX F

Role of Faith-Inspired Institutions in Tertiary Education

The analysis of the role of faith-inspired institutions or FIIs (we use here the term FIIs, given that tertiary education providers are not typically considered as "schools") in education service delivery in this study is focused on primary and secondary schools for two main reasons. First, this is where the bulk of students are enrolled. Second, it is likely that faith plays a larger role in the choice made by households about where to send their children at the primary and secondary levels given that these are formative years. At the tertiary level, the academic or professional credentials and the cost structure of universities are likely to be the driving forces behind the choice of institution to attend. Still, FIIs do play a role in tertiary education in many countries (as well as in technical and vocational education and training or TVET, but good data on TVET are harder to come by in national multipurpose surveys). Therefore, it is interesting to replicate the work done for primary and secondary schooling at the tertiary level. This appendix provides results from essentially the same set of multipurpose household surveys on the market share, reach to the poor, cost, and satisfaction of students with the tertiary education that they receive, again comparing public, faith-inspired, and private secular institutions. It is important to note that the number of observations in the household surveys on which the statistics provided in this appendix are based is often small, given that only a small proportion of students reach tertiary education in most Sub-Saharan Africa. But because the results essentially confirm à priori expectations, it is worthwhile to present the data.

Table F.1 suggests that the market share of FIIs is relatively small in the countries listed. In a few countries, the market share appears to be zero, and the highest market share is observed for Kenya, at 8.4 percent. Thus, even if some countries where the market share of FIIs might be higher are not included here, the market share of FIIs at the tertiary level tends to be low on average. In addition, in most countries (Ghana, Swaziland, and Zambia are exceptions), the market share for FIIs is higher in urban than in rural areas. Also, the market share of private secular providers tends to be larger than that of FIIs, and often

Table F.1 Market Share of Various Types of Providers, Tertiary Level
percent

	National	Urban	Rural		National	Urban	Rural
	Burkina, 2007				Kenya, 2005		
Public	81.2	80.9	100.0	Public	52.8	49.2	56.6
Faith-inspired	1.0	1.0	—	Faith-inspired	8.8	9.2	8.4
Private secular	17.8	18.0	—	Private secular	38.4	41.6	35.0
Total	100.0	100.0	100.0	Total	100.0	100.0	100.0
	Burundi, 2006				Zambia, 2004		
Public	49.4	40.2	68.9	Public	67.0	64.1	80.6
Faith-inspired	0.4	0.6	—	Faith-inspired	2.6	2.4	3.4
Private secular	50.2	59.2	31.1	Private secular	30.4	33.5	16.0
Total	100.0	100.0	100.0	Total	100.0	100.0	100.0
	Cameroon, 2007				Congo, Rep., 2005		
Public	88.1	87.4	94.4	Public	67.3	67.3	—
Faith-inspired	1.8	1.8	1.8	Faith-inspired	1.3	1.3	—
Private secular	10.1	10.9	3.8	Private secular	31.4	31.4	—
Total	100.0	100.0	100.0	Total	100.0	100.0	—
	Ghana, 2003				Nigeria 2003/04		
Public	93.4	93.2	94.2	Public	92.1	91.3	95.3
Faith-inspired	1.7	1.3	3.8	Faith-inspired	0.2	0.3	0.0
Private secular	4.9	5.5	2.1	Private secular	7.7	8.4	4.7
Total	100.0	100.0	100.0	Total	100.0	100.0	100.0
	Ghana, 2005/06				Niger, 2007		
Public	88.0	86.9	91.8	Public	49.8	49.5	100.0
Faith-inspired	3.5	2.9	5.9	Faith-inspired	—	—	—
Private secular	8.5	10.2	2.2	Private secular	50.2	50.6	—
Total	100.0	100.0	100.0	Total	100.0	100.0	100.0
	Senegal, 2005				Mali, 2006		
Public	74.7	74.0	95.3	Public	83.5	82.4	90.8
Faith-inspired	2.5	2.5	—	Faith-inspired	—	—	—
Private secular	22.9	23.4	4.7	Private secular	16.5	17.6	9.2
Total	100.0	100.0	100.0	Total	100.0	100.0	100.0
	Swaziland, 2009/10				Uganda, 2010		
Public	51.3	42.9	56.5	Public	52.8	41.8	65.6
Faith-inspired	4.5	2.4	5.9	Faith-inspired	5.0	5.9	3.9
Private secular	44.2	54.7	37.6	Private secular	42.2	52.3	30.6
Total	100.0	100.0	100.0	Total	100.0	100.0	100.0

Source: Tsimpo and Wodon 2013d.
Note: — = not available.

substantially so. Recall as shown in chapter 4 that the market share of FIIs in education provision at the primary level was slightly larger than that of private secular providers, and that private secular providers had on average a slightly larger market share than FIIs at the secondary level. Here private secular providers have a much larger market share than FIIs at the tertiary level, even if in most countries, the largest player remains the public sector.

Table F.2 provides data on benefit incidence. Because few students at the tertiary level are from the bottom three quintiles of welfare, those quintiles have been aggregated together. The main finding is that a large majority of students attending tertiary education belong to the top quintile of well-being, as expected. This is true for all types of providers (in the case of Ghana, the issue of different benefit

Table F.2 Benefit Incidence by Type of Provider, Tertiary Level
percent

	Welfare quintile					Welfare quintile			
	Q1–Q3	Q4	Q5	Total		Q1–Q3	Q4	Q5	Total
	Burkina, 2007					Kenya, 2005			
Public	—	7.7	92.3	100.0	Public	21.7	20.3	58.0	100.0
Faith-inspired	—	—	100.0	100.0	Faith-inspired	31.9	3.6	64.4	100.0
Private secular	—	5.6	94.4	100.0	Private secular	23.9	18.5	57.6	100.0
Total	—	7.2	92.8	100.0	Total	23.4	18.2	58.4	100.0
	Burundi, 2006					Zambia, 2004			
Public	31.3	9.6	59.2	100.0	Public	17.1	18.5	64.4	100.0
Faith-inspired	—	—	100.0	100.0	Faith-inspired	32.7	5.1	62.3	100.0
Private secular	4.3	11.1	84.6	100.0	Private secular	8.3	11.8	80.0	100.0
Total	17.6	10.3	72.1	100.0	Total	14.8	16.1	69.1	100.0
	Cameroon, 2007					Congo, Rep., 2005			
Public	6.1	19.6	74.4	100.0	Public	39.9	26.8	33.3	100.0
Faith-inspired	—	18.0	82.0	100.0	Faith-inspired	89.6	—	10.4	100.0
Private secular	4.0	7.2	88.9	100.0	Private secular	36.7	28.1	35.2	100.0
Total	5.7	18.3	76.0	100.0	Total	39.6	26.9	33.6	100.0
	Ghana, 2003					Nigeria 2003/04			
Public	36.1	29.8	34.1	100.0	Public	18.4	24.4	57.2	100.0
Faith-inspired	45.1	46.8	8.1	100.0	Faith-inspired	—	—	100.0	100.0
Private secular	10.9	53.5	35.6	100.0	Private secular	15.0	17.2	67.8	100.0
Total	35.0	31.3	33.7	100.0	Total	18.1	23.8	58.1	100.0
	Ghana, 2005/06					Niger, 2007			
Public	20.8	15.1	64.1	100.0	Public	—	18.3	81.7	100.0
Faith-inspired	—	28.1	72.0	100.0	Faith-inspired	—	—	—	—
Private secular	8.0	15.3	76.6	100.0	Private secular	4.4	7.1	88.6	100.0
Total	19.0	15.6	65.4	100.0	Total	2.2	12.7	85.1	100.0
	Senegal, 2005					Mali, 2006			
Public	12.4	21.0	66.6	100.0	Public	15.8	25.8	58.4	100.0
Faith-inspired	0.7	—	99.3	100.0	Faith-inspired	—	—	—	—
Private secular	2.6	2.7	94.8	100.0	Private secular	—	3.4	96.6	100.0
Total	9.8	16.3	73.9	100.0	Total	13.2	22.1	64.7	100.0
	Swaziland, 2009/10					Uganda, 2010			
Public	19.4	34.3	46.4	100.0	Public	11.8	9.7	78.4	100.0
Faith-inspired	—	—	100.0	100.0	Faith-inspired	11.4	19.9	68.7	100.0
Private secular	9.5	16.0	74.5	100.0	Private secular	9.9	7.8	82.4	100.0
Total	14.1	24.6	61.3	100.0	Total	11.0	9.4	79.6	100.0

Source: Tsimpo and Wodon 2013d.
Note: — = not available.

incidence results obtained with the Core Welfare Indicators Questionnaire [CWIQ] and Ghana Living Standard Survey, Fifth Round [GLSS5] surveys comes up again). In addition, in some of the countries, private secular providers tend to reach slightly better the fourth and first three quintiles than is the case for FIIs, which may be related to the higher concentration of students located in urban areas in the clientele of FIIs, as mentioned earlier. However, sample sizes are small, especially in the bottom quintiles, and especially for FIIs given their smaller market share, so that the results for lower quintiles for FIIs may not be very robust at the country level. What seems robust as a broad conclusion is the fact that whether tertiary education providers are faith-inspired, private secular, or public institutions, they do not tend to reach the poor much in all of the countries considered.

What about cost? The results are provided in local currencies in table F.3. Again, the most reliable results are those obtained for the sample as a whole, as opposed to by quintile, or location. As expected, private secular providers tend

Table F.3 Cost of Tertiary Education by Type of Provider, Local Currencies

	Location		Welfare quintile			
	Urban	Rural	Q1–Q3	Q4	Q5	Total
			Burundi, 2006			
Public	36,307	5,567	8,088	—	32,400	22,554
Faith-inspired	—	—	—	—	—	—
Private secular	90,384	55,119	6,000	4,500	97,678	83,373
Total	68,116	20,969	7,829	2,737	69,954	52,984
			Cameroon, 2007			
Public	70,804	59,331	53,743	63,008	72,588	69,554
Faith-inspired	384,789	305,000	—	652,295	315,730	376,270
Private secular	384,826	815,000	325,000	249,512	417,760	402,036
Total	110,481	94,082	72,655	80,605	118,391	108,810
			Ghana, 2005/06			
Public	1,443,721	1,289,946	1,264,566	1,440,402	1,449,144	1,409,435
Faith-inspired	721,861	3,200,000	—	889,058	1,888,333	1,608,040
Private secular	1,293,348	—	1,316,445	—	1,454,707	1,220,427
Total	1,407,487	1,374,301	1,266,432	1,284,846	1,466,811	1,400,400
			Swaziland, 2009/10			
Public	2,074	1,583	1,532	989	2,385	1,742
Faith-inspired	119	2,963	—	—	2,381	2,381
Private secular	4,982	3,411	972	1,880	5,059	4,163
Total	3,617	2,351	1,366	1,245	3,823	2,841
			Kenya, 2005			
Public	18,225	17,289	8,798	14,708	22,133	17,734
Faith-inspired	14,213	11,221	3,653	13,861	17,302	12,818
Private secular	18,495	8,629	6,741	7,001	19,427	14,094
Total	17,968	13,744	7,374	11,677	20,639	15,903

table continues next page

Table F.3 Cost of Tertiary Education by Type of Provider, Local Currencies *(continued)*

	Location		Welfare quintile			
	Urban	Rural	Q1–Q3	Q4	Q5	Total
	Nigeria 2003/04					
Public	18,618	14,244	10,883	16,313	20,553	17,737
Faith-inspired	16,000	—	—	—	16,000	16,000
Private secular	24,168	26,556	10,210	18,254	29,187	24,453
Total	19,079	14,824	10,840	16,421	21,312	18,250
	Uganda, 2010					
Public	1,243,609	884,634	313,612	897,834	1,291,877	1,095,351
Faith-inspired	951,616	800,162	300,000	535,889	130,0913	897,704
Private secular	2,165,193	1,867,061	744,743	1,757,149	2,238,833	2,077,784
Total	1,730,305	1,292,881	459,780	1,176,364	1,806,479	1,577,287

Source: Tsimpo and Wodon 2013d.
Note: — = not available.

to be more costly than public institutions, although this does not seem to be the case in Ghana and Kenya. The differences between FIIs and private secular providers tend to be smaller, and in all countries except Ghana, the average cost for FIIs is lower than for private secular institutions. Of course, cost may depend on the type of tertiary education acquired, but the data do not permit such differentiation. Thus the data suggest that FIIs are in general more expensive than public institutions, but less expensive than private secular institutions, as observed for primary and secondary education in chapter 6.

Finally, what about the satisfaction of students with the education received? The results are provided in table F.4. As for cost, the results appear to be in line with what was observed for primary and secondary education, in that satisfaction levels obtained by FIIs tend to be higher than those obtained by public institutions, and somewhat close to those obtained by private secular institutions. The same caveat as to small sample sizes applies, so one should be careful not to derive too much from the results, especially in the countries listed that have limited shares of students in tertiary institutions that are faith inspired and also limited sample sizes (the main exception being the large Ghana 2003 CWIQ survey). But the results confirm what was obtained for other levels of education, as well as anecdotal evidence. Thus, to conclude, while the market share of FIIs at the tertiary level appears to be lower than is the case for primary and secondary education (with the market share of private secular institutions being higher at that level), it is clear than the incidence of the benefits of tertiary education is highly titled towards the top quintile for all types of providers and all countries. In addition, the cost and satisfaction patterns observed for FIIs and private secular institutions mirror what is happening at the lower levels of education, that is FIIs are more expensive than public institutions, but often less expensive than private secular institutions, and they tend to have higher satisfaction rates among their students than public institutions, as is the case for private secular providers.

Table F.4 Satisfaction with Tertiary Education by Type of Provider

percent

	Location		Welfare quintile			
	Urban	Rural	Q1–Q3	Q4	Q5	Total
Burkina, 2007						
Public	59.5	44.1	—	83.9	57.2	59.2
Faith-inspired	100.0	—	—	—	100.0	100.0
Private secular	87.8	—	—	45.8	90.3	87.8
Total	65.0	44.1	—	78.6	63.6	64.7
Burundi, 2006						
Public	76.2	54.2	52.6	8.3	83.0	64.9
Faith-inspired	—	—	—	—	—	—
Private secular	72.1	24.6	0.0	0.0	74.3	61.7
Total	73.6	45.0	46.1	3.5	77.6	63.3
Ghana, 2003						
Public	71.59	75.55	75.2	70.0	71.0	72.2
Faith-inspired	93.28	83.98	92.2	95.4	46.5	90.0
Private secular	85.97	100.00	87.2	88.7	84.1	86.9
Total	72.66	76.38	75.8	72.2	71.6	73.3
Senegal, 2005						
Public	75.3	56.8	65.4	63.2	79.9	74.6
Faith-inspired	100.0	—	100.0	—	100.0	100.0
Private secular	78.2	100.0	73.0	66.5	78.8	78.3
Total	76.6	58.8	66.0	63.3	80.2	76.1
Congo, Rep., 2005						
Public	17.2	—	16.2	25.4	11.8	17.2
Faith-inspired	56.3	—	51.2	—	100.0	56.3
Private secular	59.9	—	46.5	71.6	64.5	59.9
Total	31.1	—	26.1	40.6	29.5	31.1
Niger, 2007						
Public	90.6	100.0	—	86.8	91.6	90.7
Faith-inspired	—	—	—	—	—	—
Private secular	98.4	—	100.0	100.0	98.2	98.4
Total	94.5	100.0	100.0	90.5	95.0	94.6
Mali, 2006						
Public	49.5	38.7	40.6	50.2	49.1	48.0
Faith-inspired	—	—	—	—	—	—
Private secular	5.5	34.9	—	37.2	6.5	7.5
Total	41.8	38.3	40.6	49.9	38.6	41.3

Source: Tsimpo and Wodon 2013d.
Note: — = not available.

APPENDIX G

Detailed Regression Estimates

This appendix provides the detailed regression results for the analysis commented upon in the main text. In chapter 6, the text refers to regressions estimated on the correlates of the cost of education in Ghana. The full results are in tables G.1 with bootstrapping. In chapter 7, the text refers to regressions estimated on the correlates of the subjective perceptions of literacy and numeracy for 10–15 years old in primary schools in Ghana in 2005/06, again with bootstrapping. The full results are in table G.2. In chapter 6, the text refers to regressions on school enrollment for children with disability. The full results are in table G.3.

Table G.1 Correlates of the Cost of Education for Households, Ghana, 2005/06

	Tobit with bootstrapping	
	Coefficient	t-value
Type of school (instr.; Ref.: Public)		
Religious school	−6.60	−0.865
Private secular school	4.90***	3.388
Level of well-being and interaction effects		
2nd quintile	0.21	0.967
3rd quintile	0.41*	1.789
4th quintile	0.68***	2.760
Top quintile	1.25***	4.129
Religious × Quintile 2	6.04	0.851
Religious × Quintile 3	5.79	0.749
Religious × Quintile 4	8.35	1.099
Religious × Quintile 5	8.35	1.090
Private × Quintile 2	−1.50	−0.993
Private × Quintile 3	−1.77	−1.215
Private × Quintile 4	−2.56*	−1.774
Private × Quintile 5	−3.46**	−2.392

table continues next page

Table G.1 Correlates of the Cost of Education for Households, Ghana, 2005/06 *(continued)*

	Tobit with bootstrapping	
	Coefficient	t-value
Location		
Urban (Ref: Rural)	0.77***	5.278
Western (Ref: Greater Accra)	−0.83***	−3.215
Central	−0.39	−1.385
Volta	−0.76**	−2.476
Eastern	−0.36	−1.388
Ashanti	−0.72***	−2.877
Brong Ahafo	−0.33	−1.208
Northern	−2.10***	−5.971
Upper East	−1.79***	−4.884
Upper West	−1.66***	−3.471
Gender and age of the head		
Male	−0.02	−0.263
Age of the head	−0.00	−1.360
Religion of the head		
Christian	0.04	0.173
Spiritualist	0.29	0.880
Muslim	0.05	0.191
Traditional	−0.52	−1.190
Grade		
Primary 2nd year	0.27***	2.812
Primary 3rd year	0.19*	1.827
Primary 4th year	0.31***	2.789
Primary 5th year	0.42***	3.302
Primary 6th year	0.58***	3.768
Characteristics of the child		
Male child	0	0.0444
Oldest child	0.05	0.713
Father living in the household	0.09	0.933
Mother living in the household	0.05	0.487
Child aged 7–10 (Ref: 5–6 years old)	−1.24**	−2.471
Child aged 11–15 (Ref: 5–6 years old)	−1.20**	−2.368
Lambda (Mills)	1.22*	1.893
Constant	1.90***	35.74

Source: Estimation based on GLSS5 2005/06 survey. See Adoho and Wodon 2013b.
Note: * significance at 10 percent level, ** at the five percent level, and *** at the one percent level.

Detailed Regression Estimates

Table G.2 Correlates of Perceptions of Literacy and Numeracy, 10–15 Years Old (Primary), Ghana 2005/06

	Can read in English (dF/dX)		Can write in English (dF/dX)		Can do written calculation (dF/dX)	
	No instrument	Instrument	No instrument	Instrument	No instrument	Instrument
Type of school (Ref.: Public)						
Religious	−0.048	−0.294	−0.348	−0.082*	0.005	0.007
Private	0.202*	0.205*	0.257***	0.186**	0.042*	0.037
Religious and urban	0.124*	0.124*	0.097	0.109	0.032	0.034
Private and urban	−0.13***	0.105***	0.079	−0.108*	−0.074	−0.003
Urban	0.125***	0.099***	0.108***	0.133***	0.029**	0.023*
Region (Ref.: Greater Accra)						
Western	−0.119	−0.095	−0.072	−0.094	−0.052	−0.045
Central	−0.199**	−0.175**	−0.114*	−0.138	−0.017	−0.012
Volta	−0.294***	−0.272***	−0.245***	−0.269***	−0.034	−0.028
Eastern	−0.264***	−0.231***	−0.234***	−0.269***	−0.025	−0.019
Ashanti	−0.19**	−0.172**	−0.101*	−0.124	0.000	0.003
Brong Ahafo	−0.187**	−0.161**	−0.131**	−0.164*	−0.049	−0.044
Northern	−0.125	−0.091	−0.135**	−0.181	−0.146***	−0.137**
Upper East	−0.062	−0.032	−0.077	−0.121	−0.082*	−0.076
Upper West	−0.020	−0.008	−0.043	−0.067	−0.026	−0.023
Level of well-being (Ref.: 1st quintile)						
Quintile 2	−0.006	−0.001	−0.021	−0.025	−0.001	−0.001
Quintile 3	0.030	0.032	0.008	0.006	0.001	0.000
Quintile 4	0.082**	0.088**	0.051	0.049	0.023*	0.022
Quintile 5	0.098***	0.113***	0.108**	0.092**	0.032**	0.032*
Faith affiliation (Ref.: No religion)						
Christian	0.077	0.073	0.066	0.070	0.057**	0.057**
Spiritualist	0.061	0.060	0.077	0.082	0.017	0.018
Muslim	0.012	0.017	0.016	0.013	0.033	0.034*
Traditional	0.062	0.049	0.051	0.067	0.032	0.032
Sex, rank, and age of the child						
Boy	0.043**	0.04**	0.039**	0.042**	0.023***	0.024***
Child is oldest in household	−0.001	0.001	−0.009	−0.008	0.005	0.006
Child is between 11 and 15 years of age	0.028	0.025	0.023	0.024	0.018	0.019*
Presence of child's parents at home						
Father is living in the household	−0.024	−0.028	−0.040	−0.032	−0.004	−0.005
Mother is living in the household	0.023	0.022	0.033	0.032	0.025*	0.024*
Time use of the child						
Time spent for housekeeping	0.001**	0.001**	0.001*	0.001**	0.001**	0.001**
Time spent on homework	−0.001	−0.001	0.001	0.001	−0.000	−0.000
Time to go to and back from school	0.006	0.008	0.006	0.004	0.002	0.003

table continues next page

Table G.2 Correlates of Perceptions of Literacy and Numeracy, 10–15 Years Old (Primary), Ghana 2005/06
(continued)

	Can read in English (dF/dX)		Can write in English (dF/dX)		Can do written calculation (dF/dX)	
	No instrument	Instrument	No instrument	Instrument	No instrument	Instrument
Payment of education fees						
Father pays the most	0.031	0.036	0.020	0.014	−0.007	−0.006
Mother pays the most	0.002	0.005	−0.020	−0.023	−0.029	−0.029
Both parent pay the most	0.018	0.028	−0.007	−0.018	0.006	0.007
Grade (Ref.: 2nd year)						
Primary 3rd year	0.156***	0.156***	0.16***	0.159***	0.031***	0.032***
Primary 4th year	0.208***	0.209***	0.257***	0.256***	0.041***	0.042***
Primary 5th year	0.266***	0.267***	0.327***	0.326***	0.061***	0.062***
Primary 6th year	0.312***	0.313***	0.384***	0.384***	0.069***	0.07***
Education of head (Ref.: No education)						
Primary	0.018	0.019	0.020	0.019	−0.002	−0.002
JSSS/M	0.064**	0.064**	0.042	0.039	−0.001	−0.001
SSS/S/U/L	0.063	0.07	0.081	0.074	−0.018	−0.019
Voc/tech/compu/comm/agri	0.135	0.133	0.090	0.090		
Teaching/nursing training	0.015	0.016	0.137**	0.135**	0.028	0.028
Polytech/university/other tertiary	0.096	0.096	0.049	0.057	0.006	0.007
Education of spouse (Ref.: No education)						
Primary	0.029	0.026	0.010	0.012	0.008	0.007
JSSS/M	0.084***	0.083***	0.082***	0.085***	0.023*	0.024*
Higher/other education level	0.065**	0.063**	0.044	0.049	0.023	0.023

Source: Estimation based on GLSS5 2005/06 survey. See Adoho and Wodon (2013c).
Note: * indicates statistical significance at the 10 percent level, ** at the 5 percent level, and *** at the 1 percent level.

Table G.3 Correlates of School Enrollment and Impact of Disability, Ghana 2003

	Model 1			Model 2			Model 3		
	Religious	Private	Not enrolled	Religious	Private	Not enrolled	Religious	Private	Not enrolled
Disability Status									
Child is disabled	0.0109*	−0.0048	0.1270***	0.0134*	0.0052	0.0351	0.0127*	0.0053	0.0504**
Severity of disability (Ref.: Mild)									
Moderate				−0.0045	0.0031	0.0735**	−0.0048	0.0034	0.0725**
Severe				−0.0029	−0.0647***	0.2675***	−0.0028	−0.0640***	0.2655***
Disability and poverty interaction									
Disabled and in the first two quintiles							0.0035	−0.0077	−0.0478*
Sex of the child (Ref.: Female)									
Male	−0.0016	0.0050***	−0.0459***	−0.0016	0.0050***	−0.0459***	−0.0016	0.0050***	−0.0459***
Disability and sex interaction									
Child is Male and disabled	−0.0249**	−0.0071	−0.0100	−0.0247**	−0.0058	−0.0118	−0.0251**	−0.0057	−0.0074
Age of the child									
Age of the child	0.0057***	0.0087***	−0.1601***	0.0057***	0.0087***	−0.1604***	0.0057***	0.0087***	−0.1604***
Age of the child squared	−0.0004***	−0.0007***	0.0077***	−0.0004***	−0.0008***	0.0077***	−0.0004***	−0.0008***	0.0077***
Nearest prim. school (Ref.: < 15')									
15–29 minutes	−0.0024	−0.0011	0.0421***	−0.0024	−0.0012	0.0425***	−0.0024	−0.0012	0.0425***
30–44 minutes	−0.0079***	−0.0070**	0.0806***	−0.0079***	−0.0070**	0.0808***	−0.0079***	−0.0070**	0.0808***
45+ minutes	−0.0110***	−0.0040	0.1976***	−0.0110***	−0.0040	0.1976***	−0.0110***	−0.0040	0.1975***
Residence (Ref.: Rural)									
Urban	−0.0282***	−0.0499***	0.0518***	−0.0282***	−0.0499***	0.0517***	−0.0282***	−0.0499***	0.0517***
Region (Ref.: Greater Accra)									
Western	0.0015	−0.0208***	−0.0191*	0.0015	−0.0206***	−0.0201**	0.0015	−0.0206***	−0.0200**
Central	0.0195***	−0.0196***	−0.0478***	0.0195***	−0.0196***	−0.0477***	0.0195***	−0.0196***	−0.0477***

table continues next page

Table G.3 Correlates of School Enrollment and Impact of Disability, Ghana 2003 (continued)

	Model 1			Model 2			Model 3		
	Religious	Private	Not enrolled	Religious	Private	Not enrolled	Religious	Private	Not enrolled
Volta	0.0011	−0.0546***	0.0154	0.0012	−0.0545***	0.0149	0.0011	−0.0545***	0.0150
Eastern	0.0187***	−0.0406***	−0.0267***	0.0187***	−0.0404***	−0.0275***	0.0187***	−0.0404***	−0.0274***
Ashanti	0.0115***	−0.0230***	−0.0280***	0.0115***	−0.0229***	−0.0283***	0.0115***	−0.0229***	−0.0282***
Brong Ahafo	0.0051	−0.0261***	−0.0330***	0.0051	−0.0260***	−0.0334***	0.0051	−0.0260***	−0.0332***
Northern	0.0252***	−0.1107***	0.1444***	0.0252***	−0.1105***	0.1443***	0.0252***	−0.1105***	0.1441***
Upper east	0.0035	−0.1349***	0.0647***	0.0035	−0.1347***	0.0642***	0.0035	−0.1347***	0.0641***
Upper west	0.0659***	−0.1212***	0.0996***	0.0659***	−0.1209***	0.0992***	0.0659***	−0.1209***	0.0992***
Household demographics									
Number of children 0–4 years old	−0.0005	0.0014	0.0096***	−0.0005	0.0014	0.0096***	−0.0005	0.0014	0.0096***
Number of children 5–14 years old	−0.0006	0.0013**	0.0051***	−0.0006	0.0013**	0.0051***	−0.0006	0.0013**	0.0051***
Number of adults 15–59 years old	0.0008*	0.0036***	−0.0023**	0.0008*	0.0036***	−0.0023**	0.0008*	0.0036***	−0.0023**
Number of seniors 60+ years	−0.0041**	0.0004	−0.0052	−0.0041**	0.0004	−0.0051	−0.0041**	0.0004	−0.0050
Sex of head (Ref.: Female)									
Male	−0.0037**	−0.0046***	0.0427***	−0.0037**	−0.0047***	0.0431***	−0.0037**	−0.0047***	0.0432***
Age of household head									
Age of head	−0.0006*	−0.0006*	−0.0013*	−0.0006*	−0.0006*	−0.0013*	−0.0006*	−0.0006*	−0.0013*
Age of head squared	0**	0	0	0**	0	0	0**	0	0
Employment of head (Ref.: Unemployed)									
Public	−0.0026	0.0057*	−0.0900***	−0.0025	0.0057*	−0.0904***	−0.0026	0.0057*	−0.0903***
Private formal	0.0011	0.0180***	−0.0218**	0.0011	0.0180***	−0.0220**	0.0011	0.0180***	−0.0219**
Private informal	−0.0082***	−0.0024	0.0006	−0.0082***	−0.0024	0.0006	−0.0082***	−0.0024	0.0006
Self-agriculture	0.0030	−0.0586**	0.0328	0.0030	−0.0586**	0.0332	0.0030	−0.0586**	0.0333
Self-other	0.0108	−0.0182	−0.0534	0.0108	−0.0187	−0.0532	0.0109	−0.0187	−0.0533
Other	−0.0083	0.0276***	−0.0881***	−0.0083	0.0276***	−0.0872***	−0.0083	0.0276***	−0.0866***

table continues next page

Table G.3 Correlates of School Enrollment and Impact of Disability, Ghana 2003 *(continued)*

	Model 1			Model 2			Model 3		
	Religious	Private	Not enrolled	Religious	Private	Not enrolled	Religious	Private	Not enrolled
Education of head (Ref.: No education)									
Primary 1–3	0.0051	0.0209***	−0.0928***	0.0051	0.0210***	−0.0932***	0.0051	0.0210***	−0.0932***
Primary 4–6	0.0054*	0.0158***	−0.0729***	0.0054*	0.0159***	−0.0730***	0.0054*	0.0158***	−0.0731***
JSS 1–3	−0.0003	0.0209***	−0.0828***	−0.0004	0.0209***	−0.0826***	−0.0004	0.0209***	−0.0825***
Middle 1–4	0.0126***	0.0311***	−0.1474***	0.0126***	0.0311***	−0.1477***	0.0126***	0.0310***	−0.1478***
SSS 1–3	0.0067	0.0533***	−0.1458***	0.0067	0.0532***	−0.1451***	0.0067	0.0532***	−0.1451***
Secondary 1–5	0.0183***	0.0536***	−0.2009***	0.0183***	0.0535***	−0.2003***	0.0183***	0.0535***	−0.2006***
Lower/upper	0.0136**	0.0488***	−0.1413***	0.0135**	0.0487***	−0.1402***	0.0135**	0.0487***	−0.1405***
Voc/tech/com/agr.	0.0249***	0.0461***	−0.1712***	0.0249***	0.0461***	−0.1713***	0.0249***	0.0461***	−0.1714***
Teaching training	0.0050	0.0315***	−0.1979***	0.0050	0.0314***	−0.1969***	0.0050	0.0314***	−0.1970***
Nursing	0.0197**	0.0608***	−0.1062***	0.0197**	0.0605***	−0.1049***	0.0197**	0.0605***	−0.1050***
Tertiary	0.0187***	0.0607***	−0.1505***	0.0186***	0.0605***	−0.1498***	0.0187***	0.0605***	−0.1501***
Level of well-being (Ref.: 1st quintile)									
2nd quintile	0.0050***	0.0278***	−0.0765***	0.0050***	0.0277***	−0.0762***	0.0050***	0.0277***	−0.0771***
3rd quintile	0.0025	0.0441***	−0.0875***	0.0025	0.0440***	−0.0872***	0.0025	0.0439***	−0.0881***
4th quintile	0.0036	0.0597***	−0.0882***	0.0036	0.0596***	−0.0877***	0.0036	0.0595***	−0.0886***
Top quintile	0.0113***	0.0654***	−0.0593***	0.0113***	0.0654***	−0.0596***	0.0114***	0.0653***	−0.0604***
Constant	−0.0768***	−0.0608***	0.6473***	−0.0768***	−0.0612***	0.6493***	−0.0769***	−0.0611***	0.6499***
Number of observations	79452	79452	79452	79452	79452	79452	79452	79452	79452

Source: Estimation based on GLSS5 2005/06 survey. See Adoho and Wodon 2013a.
Note: * indicates statistical significance at the 10 percent level, ** at the 5 percent level, and *** at the 1 percent level.

APPENDIX H

Illegitimate Fees in Service Delivery

The issue of illegitimate fees or petty corruption in service delivery is widespread in developing countries, including in Sub-Saharan Africa. In principle, when households are asked in surveys how much they spend on education, this should include any illegitimate fees that they may have had to provide to service providers. However, most surveys do not have information that permits the estimation of the magnitude of such illegitimate fees separately from other expenditures. This section provides two examples of analysis related to petty corruption. The first from Sierra Leone suggests that illegitimate fees may be widespread, including in education service delivery. The second from Cameroon suggests that the likelihood of having to pay illegitimate fees may be (slightly) less frequent among users of services provided by faith-inspired schools (FISs), as compared to public and other private secular education providers.

Consider first the case of Sierra Leone. Through a collaboration between the government and the World Bank Institute on governance, three separate surveys were implemented in 2003 to measure the extent of corruption. The three surveys are based on interviews with respectively 1,800 households, 600 firms, and 590 public officials. In this appendix, only the household survey is used. One of the questions asked to households in the survey directly relates to the "gratifications" paid by households when using a range of services. While gratifications may not necessarily represent corruption, they are typically not to be paid to service providers or their staffs. It is however possible that in some cases, gratifications represent legitimate payments. The health sector comes to mind. Given that in the survey 90 percent of users declare paying gratifications for public health services, it could be that part of this is related to healthcare cost recovery (public expenditures on healthcare in Sierra Leone are low, focusing mostly on salaries so that cost recovery is often used for basic supplies and medication). Thus, in the case of healthcare, it may not be appropriate to label these payments as corruption, and it remains an open issue as to whether these payments should be abolished or not. Yet in many sectors, the payments considered by households as gratifications are likely to be illegitimate.

In order to assess the frequency and level of these gratifications, three questions in the survey can be used: *(1) During the last year, approximately how many times has anyone in your household contacted the institution concerning the services that the public institution provides?; (2) Of these total contacts, on average, how many times were you required to pay a gratification?; and (3) how much did you have to pay as gratification each time you made official payments in Leones? (in equivalent value if it took the form of gift or other favor?)* These three questions are asked for many services, most of which are provided by the public sector or quasi-public providers. There is also a follow up question worded as follows: "Given the present situation, many have told us candidly that they are obliged to make gratifications to public officials. How much do you think is typically spent each month on gratifications to public officials?" This information is asked both as an amount, and as a percentage of total household income. There are thus two different ways to compute the level of gratifications paid by households, first by summing up all gratifications declared to be paid for the various services used by the household, and second by using the aggregate approximate amount paid in gratifications declared by the household. It is likely that the first measure will lead to a higher estimate of the gratifications paid than the aggregate measure provided by the household, given that when declaring an aggregate value, households may well forget some of the gratifications that they have had to pay.

It turns out that the amounts of gratifications that have to be paid by households to benefit from public services are not negligible in comparison with their total income. Table H.1 provides the estimates of the amounts paid as a share of the total income of the household. In order to not have extreme (and probably erroneous) values affecting the estimation, for any specific service or for all services as a whole, it has been assumed that a household cannot and has not paid more than 25 percent of its income for gratifications. In the first row of the table, the share of total income allocated to gratifications is computed using the summation approach by adding all the gratifications paid for different services. The data suggest that 5.4 percent of total income may be used for gratification, but the proportion is much higher for the poor (at 11.9 percent) than for the nonpoor (at 4.0 percent). In the second row of the table, the same procedure is used, but for those households for which there is a missing value as to their total income in the survey, an imputed income was estimated using a simple regression analysis. The estimates are similar, with gratifications representing 5.9 percent of total income on average, again with higher estimates for the poor than the nonpoor. Finally, when using the summary question on all gratifications paid, gratifications represent 2.9 percent of total household income, and in this case differences between the poor and the nonpoor are small. Overall, these amounts from 3 percent to 6 percent of total income are not negligible, especially for the poor. Given the limited ability to pay such gratifications among the poor, the issue is serious.

There are differences between services in the shares of individuals using the services who have to pay gratifications. The shares of household paying gratifications varies widely according to the services used. They are very high for health

Table H.1 Gratifications Paid as a Share of Total Income, Sierra Leone 2003

percent

	Mean share	Minimum value	Maximum value
	National		
Share in raw data with 25% income share cap	5.4	0.3	25.0
Share with imputed income with 25% cap	5.9	0.3	25.0
Share as overall estimate with 25% cap	2.9	0	25.0
	Nonpoor		
Share in raw data with 25% income share cap	4.0	0.3	25.0
Share with imputed income with 25% cap	4.2	0.3	25.0
Share as overall estimate with 25% cap	3.2	0	25.0
	Poor		
Share in raw data with 25% income share cap	11.9	1.3	25.0
Share with imputed income with 25% cap	11.5	1.3	25.0
Share as overall estimate with 25% cap	2.6	0	25.0

Source: Author's estimation using 2003 Sierra Leone Governance survey.

services (above 90 percent of users pay gratifications), and high as well for a wide range of other services (traffic police, other police, judges and court officials, income tax department, and so on). Except in the case of pensions, where no gratifications appear to be paid (possibly because pensions are of a fixed amount and are to be paid on regular intervals without the need to intervene), about 30 percent or more of service users pay gratification for the services. In the case of public education, gratifications are paid by almost 40 percent of the households. The amounts paid per year are highest for the income tax department and for the police (excluding the traffic police), at about 30,000 Le, and lowest for health services, at slightly more than 5,000 Le (at the time of the survey, the exchange rate was approximately Le 2,000 per US dollar). In the case of education, they are at about 10,000 Leones per household. For a typical household, the total amount paid across services almost reaches 35,000 Le per year on average. While this may not seem to be a large amount, it represents resources that households could valuably allocate to other goods and services. Given that income levels are low in Sierra Leone (two thirds of the population is poor), the burden represented by gratifications is real.

Consider now the second example, related to education service delivery in Cameroon. In the ECAM 2 survey for 2001, two questions are asked to households as to whether they have paid nonregulatory fees for education—the language is meant to identify illegitimate fees, that is petty corruption. Information is available on whether households did pay illegitimate fees, but not on the amount of fees paid. Because the survey also includes information on the types of service providers used by households, including both faith-inspired and secular private providers apart from public providers, it is feasible to assess whether the degree of petty corruption is lower among FISs than among other providers. The question is asked at the household level, and a household may have several children attending different types of school, possibly from different types of providers. Still, while it is necessary to conduct the analysis at the household rather than at the child or household member level, it remains feasible to distinguish households sending all their children to public schools, from those sending all their children to FISs or private secular schools, and those sending some children to one type of school and other children to another type of school.

The results for education are provided in table H.2. Private faith-inspired schools have the lowest proportion of households declaring paying illegitimate fees, at 15.5 percent. For private secular schools the proportion is at 17.1 percent, and for public schools it is at 20.4 percent. For households relying on a combination of schools, the proportions are even higher, but this makes sense since when using more than one type of school, the household is likely to interact with more schools and staffs, and thereby is more likely to have to pay illegitimate fees. Again, it could very well be that some of the fees are actually legitimate. Note that the probability of paying illegitimate fees tends to be higher in the higher quintiles as well as in urban areas as compared to rural areas, suggesting that the ability to pay such fees plays a role in whether fees are paid by households, which may also give better off households an advantage for their children in school (there is anecdotal evidence in the literature on the role that such illegitimate fees may play in the types of grades that a child may receive from a teacher, for example for qualifying examinations). For the purpose of this study, the data in table H.2 provide at least some evidence that the level of petty corruption in FISs may perhaps be lower than in other types of schools.

Table H.2 Share of Households Paying Illegitimate School Fees, Cameroon 2001
percent

	Quintile					Location		
	Q1	Q2	Q3	Q4	Q5	Urban	Rural	All
Public	14.1	19.1	18.2	27.4	24.2	31.1	16.0	20.4
Private faith-inspired	1.8	15.6	16.7	24.6	17.6	23.1	12.8	15.5
Private secular	16.3	5.3	26.6	20.1	16.2	19.5	10.2	17.1
Faith inspired and private secular	11.3	12.0	11.7	21.1	36.1	26.1	11.1	21.0
Public and at least one private	15.5	23.4	31.0	36.5	37.4	38.2	19.0	31.2
No children in school	2.5	1.4	4.3	6.5	7.3	8.8	4.1	5.5
All	10.4	13.2	14.7	18.5	15.4	22.9	10.5	14.9

Source: Tsimpo and Wodon 2013c.

References

Adoho, F., and Q. Wodon. 2013a. "Impact of Disability on School Enrollment: Evidence from a Large Sample Survey in Ghana. " Mimeo, World Bank, Washington, DC.

———. 2013b. "Comparing the Cost of Public, Private Secular, and Faith-Based Education Providers in Ghana." Mimeo, World Bank, Washington, DC.

———. 2013c. "Performance of Public, Private Secular, and Faith-Inspired Schools in Ghana: An Analysis based on Subjective Perceptions of Literacy and Numeracy." Mimeo, World Bank, Washington, DC.

Allcott, H., and D. E. Ortega. 2009. "The Performance of Decentralized School Systems: Evidence from Fe y Alegría in Venezuela." In *Emerging Evidence on Vouchers and Faith-Based Providers in Education: Case Studies from Africa, Latin America, and Asia*, edited by F. Barrera-Osorio, H. A. Patrinos, and Q. Wodon. Washington, DC: World Bank.

Altonji, J. G., T. E. Elder, and C. R. Taber. 2005. "An Evaluation of Instrumental Variable Strategies for Estimating the Effects of Catholic Schooling." *Journal of Human Resources* 40: 791–821.

Asadullah, M. N., N. Chaudhury, and A. Dar. 2009. "Student Achievement in Religious and Secular Secondary Schools in Bangladesh." In *Emerging Evidence on Vouchers and Faith-Based Providers in Education: Case Studies from Africa, Latin America, and Asia*, edited by H. A. P. F. Barrera-Osorio and Q. Wodon. Washington, DC: World Bank.

Backiny-Yetna, P., and Q. Wodon. 2009a. "Comparing the Private Cost of Education at Public, Private, and Faith-Based Schools in Cameroon." In *Emerging Evidence on Vouchers and Faith-Based Providers in Education: Case Studies from Africa, Latin America, and Asia*, edited by F. Barrera-Osorio, H. A. Patinos, and Q. Wodon. Washington, DC: World Bank.

———. 2009b. "Comparing the Performance of Faith-Based and Government Schools in the Democratic Republic of Congo." In *Emerging Evidence on Vouchers and Faith-Based Providers in Education: Case Studies from Africa, Latin America, and Asia*, edited by F. Barrera-Osorio, H. A. Patinos, and Q. Wodon. Washington, DC: World Bank.

Bamberger, M., ed. 2000. *Integrating Quantitative and Qualitative Research in Development Projects*. Washington, DC: World Bank.

Barrera-Osorio, F., H. A. Patrinos, and Q. Wodon, eds. 2009a. *Emerging Evidence on Vouchers and Faith-Based Providers in Education: Case Studies from Africa, Latin America, and Asia*. Washington, DC: World Bank.

———. 2009b. "Public-Private Partnerships in Education: An Overview." In *Emerging Evidence on Vouchers and Faith-Based Providers in Education: Case Studies from Africa, Latin America, and Asia*, edited by F. Barrera-Osorio, H. A. Patinos, and Q. Wodon. Washington, DC: World Bank.

Bourdieu, P., and L. J. D. Wacquant. 1992. *An Invitation to Reflexive Sociology*. Chicago: University of Chicago Press.

Bradley, T. 2009. "A Call for Clarification and Critical Analysis of the Work of Faith-Based Development Organizations (FBDOs)." *Progress in Development Studies* 2: 101–14.

Buchanan, D., D. Boddy, and J. McCalman. 1998. "Getting In, Getting On, Getting Out, and Getting Back." In *Doing Research in Organizations*, edited by A. Bryman. London: Routledge.

Clarke, G. 2006. "Faith Matters: Faith-Based Organizations, Civil Society and International Development." *Journal of International Development* 18: 835–48.

Clert, C., E. Gacitua-Mario, and Q. Wodon. 2001. "Combining Qualitative and Quantitative Methods for Policy Research on Poverty within a Social Exclusion Framework." In *Measurement and Meaning: Combining Quantitative and Qualitative Methods for the Analysis of Poverty and Social Exclusion in Latin America*, edited by E. Gacitua-Mario and Q. Wodon. World Bank Technical Paper No. 518, World Bank, Washington, DC.

Cohen-Zada, D., and W. Sander. 2008. "Religion, Religiosity and Private School Choice: Implications for Estimating the Effectiveness of Private Schools." *Journal of Urban Economics* 64: 85–100.

Cox, D., and E. Jimenez. 1990. "The Relative Effectiveness of Private and Public Schools: Evidence from Two Developing Countries." *Journal of Development Economics* 34 (1–2): 99–121.

Coulombe, H., and Q. Wodon. 2007. *Poverty, Livelihoods and Access to Basic Services in Ghana*. Washington, DC: World Bank.

De Lange, A. 2007. *Deprived Children and Education—Namentenga, Burkina Faso*. Amsterdam: IREWOC—International Research on Working Children.

Deneulin, S., and C. Rakodi. 2011. "Revisiting Religion: Development Studies Thirty Years on." *World Development* 39: 45–54.

Dimmock, F., J. Olivier, and Q. Wodon. 2012. "Half a Century Young: The Christian Health Associations in Africa." In *The Role of Faith-Inspired Health Care Providers in Sub-Saharan Africa and Public-Private Partnerships: Strengthening the Evidence for Faith-Inspired Engagement in Africa*. Vol. 1. HNP Discussion Paper, World Bank, Washington, DC.

Doupe, A. 2005. *Partnerships between Churches and People Living with HIV/AIDS Organizations*. Geneva: World Council of Churches.

Dovlo, E. 2005. "Religion in the Public Sphere: Challenges and Opportunities in Ghanaian Lawmaking 1989–2004." *Brigham Young University Law Review* 2005: 629–58.

Epple, D., and R. E. Romano. 1998. "Competition between Private and Public Schools, Vouchers, and Peer-Group Effects." *The American Economic Review* 88 (1): 33–62.

Evans, W., and R. Schwab. 1995. "Finishing High School and Starting College: Do Catholic Schools Make a Difference?" *Quarterly Journal of Economics* 110: 941–74.

Gemignani, R., and Q. Wodon. 2013. "Why Drives the Choice of Faith-Inspired Schools by Households? Evidence from Burkina Faso." Mimeo, World Bank, Washington, DC.

George, J., and Q. Wodon. 2013. "Performance in Ghana's Public and Private Primary Schools." Mimeo, World Bank, Washington, DC.

González, R. A., and G. Arévalo. 2005. "Subsidized Catholic Schools in Venezuela." In *Private Education and Public Policy in Latin America*, edited by L. Wolff, J. C. Navarro, and P. González. Washington, DC: Project for Educational Revitalization in the Americas.

References

Hagberg, S. 2002. "Learning to Live or Learning to Leave? Education and Identity in Burkina Faso." *African Sociological Review* 6 (2): 28–46.

Hoxby, C. M. 1994. "Do Private Schools Provide Competition for Public Schools?" National Bureau of Economic Research Working Paper 4978, NBER, Cambridge, MA.

Hsieh, C., and M. Urquiola. 2006. "The Effects of Generalized School Choice on Achievement and Stratification: Evidence from Chile's School Voucher Program." *Journal of Public Economics* 90: 1477–1503.

Iddrisu, A. 2002. "Between Islamic and Western Secular Education in Ghana: A Progressive Integration Approach." *Journal of Muslim Minority Affairs* 22 (2): 335–50.

———. 2005. "The Growth of Islamic Learning in Northern Ghana and Its Interaction with Western Secular Education." *Africa Development* XXX (1–2): 53–67.

Jepsen, C. 2003. "The Effectiveness of Catholic Primary Schooling." *Journal of Human Resources* 38: 928–41.

Jimenez, E., and M. E. Lockheed. 1995. "Public and Private Secondary Education in Developing Countries: A Comparative Study." World Bank Discussion Paper 309, World Bank, Washington, DC.

Kitchen, M. 2002. "World Must Coordinate Efforts, End Waste, Says Wolfensohn." *UN Wire*.

Kürzinger, M. L., J. Pagnier, J. G. Kahn, R. Hampshire, T. Wakabi, and T. D. V. Dye. 2008. "Education Status among Orphans and Non-Orphans in Communities Affected by AIDS in Tanzania and Burkina Faso." *AIDS Care* 20 (6): 726–32.

LaRocque, N., and H. Patrinos. 2006. *Choice and Contracting Mechanisms in the Education Sector*. Washington, DC: World Bank.

Lipsky, A. 2011. "Evaluating the Strength of Faith: Potential Comparative Advantages of Faith-Based Organizations Providing Health Services in Sub-Saharan Africa." *Public Administration and Development* 31: 25–36.

Long, A., and N. Long, eds. 1992. *Battlefields of Knowledge: The Interlocking of Theory and Practice in Social Research and Development*. London: Routledge.

Maclure, R., B. Kabore, C. Mvoto Meyong, D. Lavan, and K. Mundy. 2007. "Civil Society and the Governance of Basic Education: Partnership or Cooptation? Burkina Faso Country Field Study." Comparative and International Development Centre, OISE/UT, Faculty of Education, University of Ottawa.

Nechyba, T. J. 2000. "Mobility, Targeting and Private School Vouchers." *American Economic Review* 90 (1): 130–46.

Neuman, W. L. 1999. *Social Research Methods: Qualitative and Quantitative Approaches*. Chicago: Allyn & Bacon.

Nouve, K., J. Kafando, A. Savadogo, D. Sebre, C. Tsimpo, and Q. Wodon. 2009. "Dynamique de la pauvreté sur base des actifs et des perceptions des ménages au Burkina Faso de 2003 à 2007." *Perspective Afrique* 4 (1–3): Article 2.

Nouve, K., Y. Bambio, S. Kabore, and Q. Wodon. 2010. "Risque et mesures de la pauvreté rurale au Burkina Faso." *Perspective Afrique* 5 (1–3): Article 5.

Olivier, J. 2011. "An FB-oh?: Mapping the Etymology of the Religious Entity Engaged in Health." In *When Religion and Health Align: Mobilizing Religious Health Assets for Transformation*, edited by J. R. Cochrane, B. Schmid, and T. Cutts. Pietermaritzburg: Cluster Publications.

Olivier, J., and Q. Wodon. 2012. "Playing Broken Telephone: Assessing Faith-Inspired Healthcare Provision in Africa." *Development in Practice* 22 (5–6): 819–34.

Ouedraogo, A. 2008. "L'Enseignement de la culture Arabe et Islamique dans le Département de Soaw, Province de Bulkiemde, Burkina Faso." *Revue de Mondes Musulmans et de la Méditerranée*.

Ouedraogo, P. 2010. "The Legacy of Christianity in West Africa, with Special Reference to Burkina Faso." *Comparative Education* 46 (3): 391–405.

Parra Osorio, J. C., and Q. Wodon. 2011. *Escuelas religiosas en América Latina: Estudios de caso sobre Fe y Alegría, Estudios del Banco Mundial*. Washington, DC: World Bank.

Ravallion M., and Q. Wodon. 2000. "Does Child Labor Displace Schooling? Evidence on Behavioral Responses to an Enrollment Subsidy." *The Economic Journal* 110: C158–75.

Reinikka, R., and J. Svensson. 2010. "Working for God? Evidence from a Change in Financing of Not-for-Profit Healthcare Providers in Uganda." *Journal of the European Economic Association* 8: 1159–78.

Rose, P. 2009. "NGO Provision of Basic Education: Alternative or Complementary Service Delivery to Support Access to the Excluded? *Compare: A Journal of Comparative and International Education* 392: 219–33.

Saul, M. 1984. "The Quranic School Farm and Child Labour in Upper Volta." *Africa: Journal of the International African Institute* 54 (2): 71–87.

Savas, E. S. 2000. *Privatization and Public-Private Partnerships*. New York: Chatham House Publishers.

Schmid, B., E. Thomas, J. Olivier, and J. R Cochrane. 2008. *The Contribution of Religious Entities to Health in Sub-Saharan Africa*. Cape Town: African Religious Health Assets Programme.

Shojo, M., and Q. Wodon. 2013. "Why Do Some Households Prefer Faith-Inspired Schools in Ghana?" Mimeo, World Bank, Washington, DC.

Sider, R., and H. R. Unruh. 2004. "Typology of Religious Characteristics of Social Service and Educational Organizations and Programs." *Nonprofit and Voluntary Sector Quarterly* 33: 109–34.

Sikand, Y. 2005. *Bastions of the Believers. Madrasas and Islamic Education in India*. New Delhi: Penguin.

———, ed. 2008a. *Madrasa Reforms: Indian Muslim Voices*. Bombay: Vikas Adhyayan Kendra.

———. 2008b. *Muslim Education in Contemporary India: A Classified and Annotated Bibliography*. Delhi: Hope India Publications.

———. 2009. Voices of reform in the Indian madrasa. In *The Madrasa in India: Political Activism and Transnational Linkages*, edited by F. A. Noor, Y. Sikand, and M. van Bruinessen. Amsterdam: Amsterdam University Press.

Tsimpo, C., and Q. Wodon. 2013a. "Trends in Religiosity and Religious Diversity: Results from the World Values Survey." Mimeo, World Bank, Washington, DC.

———. 2013b. "Assessing the Role of Faith-Inspired Primary and Secondary Schools in Africa: Evidence from Multi-Purpose Surveys." Mimeo, World Bank, Washington, DC.

———. 2013c. "Are Faith-Inspired Education and Healthcare Providers Less Susceptible to Corruption? Evidence from Cameroon." Mimeo, World Bank, Washington, DC.

———. 2013d. "Who Provides Tertiary Education to Whom, at What Cost, and with What Level of Satisfaction in Sub-Saharan Africa?" Mimeo, World Bank, Washington, DC.

UNESCO (United Nations Educational, Scientific and Cultural Organization). 2011. *Financing Education in Sub-Saharan Africa: Meeting the Challenges of Expansion, Equity, and Quality*. Montreal: UNESCO Institute for Statistics.

UNFPA (United Nations Population Fund). 2004. *Culture Matters: Working with Communities and Faith-Based Organizations: Case Studies from Country Programmes*. New York: United Nations Population Fund.

———. 2009. *Guidelines for Engaging Faith-Based Organizations (FBOs) as Agents of Change*. New York: The United Nations Population Fund.

Weiss, H. 2005. "Contested Historical and Geographical Narratives: Succession Disputes, Contested Land Ownership and Religious Conflicts in Northern Ghana." WOPAG-Working Papers on Ghana: Historical and Contemporary Studies Number 6, Åbo Akademi University and University of Helsinki, Finland.

Wodon, Q. 2000. "Low Income Energy Assistance and Disconnection in France." *Applied Economics Letters* 7: 775–79.

Wodon, Q., and Y. Ying. 2009. "Literacy and Numeracy in Faith-Based and Government Schools in Sierra Leone." In *Emerging Evidence on Vouchers and Faith-Based Providers in Education: Case Studies from Africa, Latin America, and Asia*, edited by F. Barrera-Osorio, H. A. Patinos, and Q. Wodon. Washington, DC: World Bank.

World Bank. 2001. *World Development Report 2000/2001: Attacking Poverty*. Washington, DC: World Bank.

———. 2004. *World Development Report 2004: Making Services Work for Poor People*. Washington, DC: World Bank.

———. 2005. *Education in the Democratic Republic of Congo: Priorities and Options for Regeneration*. Washington, DC: World Bank.

Yaro, Y. 1994. "Les stratégies scolaires des ménages au Burkina Faso." *Cahiers des Sciences Humaines* 31 (3): 675–96.

Environmental Benefits Statement

The World Bank is committed to reducing its environmental footprint. In support of this commitment, the Publishing and Knowledge Division leverages electronic publishing options and print-on-demand technology, which is located in regional hubs worldwide. Together, these initiatives enable print runs to be lowered and shipping distances decreased, resulting in reduced paper consumption, chemical use, greenhouse gas emissions, and waste.

The Publishing and Knowledge Division follows the recommended standards for paper use set by the Green Press Initiative. Whenever possible, books are printed on 50 percent to 100 percent postconsumer recycled paper, and at least 50 percent of the fiber in our book paper is either unbleached or bleached using Totally Chlorine Free (TCF), Processed Chlorine Free (PCF), or Enhanced Elemental Chlorine Free (EECF) processes.

More information about the Bank's environmental philosophy can be found at http://crinfo.worldbank.org/wbcrinfo/node/4.

www.ingramcontent.com/pod-product-compliance
Lightning Source LLC
Chambersburg PA
CBHW081939170426
43202CB00018B/2951